STOPPED WORK?
START LIVING!

*encouraging stories of
new directions in retirement*

Irene Howat

CHRISTIAN FOCUS

© Christian Focus Publications Ltd 2005

ISBN 1-84550-047-4

10 9 8 7 6 5 4 3 2 1

Printed in 2005
by
Christian Focus Publications Ltd.
Geanies House, Fearn, Tain, Ross-shire,
IV20 1TW, Scotland, Great Britain.

www.christianfocus.com

Cover design by Alister MacInnes

Printed and bound by Nørhaven Paperback A/S, Denmark

Stopped Work?
Start Living!

Contents

For
Alastair and Lilian

Introduction

The shape of Western society is changing, to the point of concern for those who manage our economies. They foresee the day when an ever-increasing number of retired people will be dependent on an ever-decreasing number of working people, and the tax implications worry them. We now live longer, and more of us can look forward to reaching our eighties and nineties than ever before. Not only that, but after retirement we have a reasonable expectation of years of good health. For some that means a round of golf a day and plenty of time to work in the garden. Others renew their passports and spend six months a year in the sun while their families at home brave the winter storms. Many retirees now work in the voluntary sector, having taken the places of the non-employed wives and mothers who used to deliver meals on wheels, run hospital transport and work in charity shops. The truth is that the words 'retired' and 'elderly' are no longer synonymous.

What an opportunity this presents for Christian service as churches realise what a valuable resource they have in their retired membership. Not only that, but many are sufficiently financially secure that they are able and willing to work without payment, or just in return for expenses. And to crown it all, some are still in their mid fifties! With a wealth of experience and wisdom behind them, they are open to serving the Lord in new and different ways. *Stopped Work? Start Living!* tells the story of retirees who, having left the work place behind them, took up the challenge of further Christian service. Hence the subtitle – this book might seriously endanger your golf. Those who contributed their stories did so in the hope of inspiring others to approach retirement as a new opportunity to serve the Lord Jesus, who gave his all on the cross for us.

Contrary to what some say, life does not begin at retirement. Consequently, the men and women whose stories are told in *Stopped Work? Start Living!* do not start their accounts in their fifties or sixties. They begin at the beginning by telling readers about their backgrounds in Scotland, England, America and Australia, how they came to know the Lord, and how they spent their working lives. And what a varied set of stories they present. Then they go on to show how the Lord surprised them by opening unexpected doors at a time in their lives when most of their friends were thinking of long lazy days of retirement.

Irene Howat

1.

FERGUS MACDONALD

I was born in 1936 in the village of Evanton in Ross-shire, which is situated about one mile inland from the western shore of Scotland's Cromarty Firth. During my formative years many of the families in the parish were churchgoing, the majority of them belonging to the Free Church of Scotland. This meant that the Free Church was the *de facto* national church, and that my father as the Free Church minister was a recognized community figure. Unfortunately it also meant that I and my two younger brothers, Alpin and Evan, were expected to be better behaved than our peers!

Given the evangelical tradition of the parish, a manse upbringing, and the strong focus on biblical teaching in both day school and Sunday School, as well as in an SU meeting run in the village by my mother, it is perhaps not surprising that I grew up with a world view that integrated the spiritual and the secular. The biblical grand narrative was absorbed twice daily at family worship. Next to the Bible, perhaps Bunyan's *Holy War* was the book that influenced me most, and I can still remember in my imagination becoming an enthusiastic supporter of Prince Immanuel in the battle for the city of Mansoul!

At the same time that very spiritual battle was raging inside me! I wanted to be accepted by my peers, but knew that in our small rural community those who publicly professed faith in Jesus Christ became 'marked' people whose lives were critically observed by others. However, the church practised 'open communion', and I remember as a boy towards the end of World War II, witnessing a moving incident when a German prisoner of war, working on local farms, was received at the Lord's Table as a brother in the Lord by the congregation, some of whom had recently lost loved ones in the war.

When I was thirteen, I, with my younger brother and six to eight other boys from the village SU group, went to Scripture Union camp. Towards the end of the week I remember thinking that if the camp were to last just a few days longer, I would not be able to hold out against the claims of Christ on my life. However, I continued to resist, and in the next couple of years I became more aware of the spiritual tug-of-war within me.

Two years later, in 1951, at the Sunday evening service of the Strathpeffer Convention, the Lord finally wore right through my resistance. Rev. George Duncan

10

– a well-known Keswick speaker – began his sermon by
quoting Revelation 3:20 (av): 'Behold I stand at the door
and knock: if any man hear my voice and open the door, I
will come in to him, and will sup with him, and he with me.'
These were familiar words. But that night my attention
was riveted when the preacher said: 'You don't need to
shut your eyes. You just need to do it!' And by the grace
of God I did! I can still recall the almost tangible sense
of God's presence at the conclusion of that service. After
the benediction the congregation didn't want to leave.
Not one soul moved! It was only some minutes after the
platform party retired that people began to move towards
the aisles and the exit.

Relevant after all!

Perhaps because as a youngster I had resented the unfair
expectations of my peers that I should somehow behave
'better' than they, I had grown up resistant to ever becoming
a minister. The first inkling of a change came during the
General Assembly of 1952, which my brothers and I
attended because my father was Moderator. Looking on
from the sidelines, and listening to debates on practical
issues, I remember thinking that being a minister might not
be as irrelevant as I had been thinking! Shortly after that I
became convinced God was calling me to the ministry. And
as the call was confirmed, it became increasingly focused on
missionary service in Peru.

In 1954, I left Dingwall Academy and went up to the
University of Edinburgh and from there to Free Church
College. On completing my theological studies, I accepted
an invitation to serve for two years as assistant minister in
Drumchapel, Glasgow. I felt it would be wise to gain some
practical experience in home mission before launching out

into cross-cultural evangelism overseas. These two years in Glasgow were a time of learning and also a time of romance, for I met Dolina in Drumchapel where we were engaged and married in 1961. It was a wrench to leave Drumchapel, but we were both convinced that the next step in the Lord's plan for us was to go to Peru.

We were stationed in Lima, where I was to be the pastor of the *San Andres* congregation, linked to the *San Andres* school which was run by the Free Church. Dolina undertook some English teaching in the primary department of the school, and to begin with I also taught a second year secondary class in English to help me access the culture and establish contact with the pupils. Greatly encouraged by the tolerance of our new Peruvian friends, we persevered in language learning, and at the end of six months I was able to preach in Spanish from a fully written text. We both made reasonably good progress in the language thereafter. However, we soon realized that learning the language was only the first hurdle! The second was learning the culture and entering into the Peruvian world of ideas.

Although, in God's providence, we spent a considerably shorter period in Peru (under five years) than we initially anticipated, they were among the most enriching years of our lives. Firstly, Peru helped us discover more of what was involved in the incarnation of the Son of God. Our entering the world of Peru and Peruvians, and finding our way in it mirrored Christ's entering into our human situation, standing alongside us and acting for us. Secondly, Peru taught us just how vital a component of the biblical message is the cry for social justice. Widespread public corruption and social injustices, hanging over from the feudal colonialism imposed by the Spanish *conquistadores* in the sixteenth century, created in me a new appreciation of the relevance and urgency of the words of Amos: 'Let justice roll on like a river, righteousness like a never-failing stream!' (Amos 5:24). Thirdly, we learned that racism can be overcome. For, while there was a glaring gap between rich and poor, the predominance of *mestizo* (mixed) blood had produced a society remarkably free from the 'pride of race'.

An international family

Shortly after returning to Scotland, I was invited to become the first minister of the new congregation that had recently been established in Cumbernauld new town in central Scotland. We both felt led to go to Cumbernauld where we spent thirteen very happy years, and where we brought up our family: Mairi-Anne and Catriona (both born in Lima), Joan and Grace (both born in Scotland) and John (whom we adopted after fostering him for several years). We found Cumbernauld a great place to bring up a family.

During our years there the population of Cumbernauld doubled, and it was exciting to participate in a vibrant society where 'the powers that be' placed a high priority on developing a sense of community. We had a wonderful congregation that genuinely and warmly welcomed visitors, and where a high proportion of members were 'active' in one way or another in mission. It was particularly pleasing to note how the attitude of the community to the congregation slowly changed from suspecting us as a 'Highland' implant to regarding us as an integral part of the local scene.

While in Cumbernauld I became Secretary of the local branch of the National Bible Society of Scotland (NBSS). Not only was I deeply committed to making the Scriptures available at home and overseas, but I saw the Bible Society as providing a meaningful axis on which the Free Church could co-operate with other churches. As secretary of the local branch I became a member of the Central Regional Council of the Bible Society which elected me to serve on the Board of Directors. By 1980 I had become Chairman of the Board, and in this capacity I was appointed to accompany Andrew Doig, the General Secretary, to the World Assembly of the United Bible Societies (UBS) meeting in Chiang Mai, Thailand in October 1981.

The Chiang Mai Assembly became one of my defining moments. I was deeply impressed by the extraordinarily strong fellowship that bound Bible Society leaders in the great enterprise of sowing the Good Seed by which the Kingdom of God comes into the lives of individuals and communities. But – coming from a relatively conservative ecclesiastical tradition – I was also somewhat disorientated by the challenge to work across Christian confessions and human cultures in order to enable the Good News to reach millions of people before it is too late. So immediately after the event I was glad of a quiet weekend when I was able to work my way prayerfully and progressively through the issues and begin to see these in a biblical and theological perspective.

A change of direction

Shortly after my return Andrew Doig intimated that he intended to retire and advised the NBSS Board to take steps to seek a new General Secretary. At first I had no thought of applying. Being involved in the Bible Society as a volunteer was a bumpy enough ride. Surely becoming a staff worker could only make the going rougher! And to leave the congregational ministry and enter into the service of the wider church ought not, I thought, to be a step lightly taken. In addition, we were very happy in Cumbernauld. But some of my close friends urged me to consider making myself available, and as Dolina and I discussed it and prayed about it, it became clear that I should do just that.

So it was that I became General Secretary of the NBSS in March 1981, and I was to continue in this post for seventeen years. I soon discovered that leading and administrating a church-related organization is very different from being a pastor of a congregation, and my early years in the job involved a steep learning curve. But I thank God that there were positive developments during my tenure, with the visibility of the Bible Society increasing among the churches and in society.

I was strongly supported by a good staff team and a very sympathetic board. Numerous new Scripture products helped churches to use the Word of God creatively in both nurture and outreach. By creatively supporting volunteers and extending the donor base, both financial income and Scripture distribution (at home and overseas) increased. Sponsoring the church censuses in 1984 and 1994 yielded data on Bible version preference and the extent of Bible use as well as attendance numbers, and incidentally gave the NBSS a research image.

In 1986 the Edinburgh Commonwealth Games Committee was persuaded to overcome their fear that placing the New Testament in the welcome pack for athletes and officials might cause offence to competitors of other faiths. These testaments made an impact: Kriss Akabusi, the hurdler, read his copy from cover to cover in the games village and says that this was a major factor in his decision to become a Christian. Some years later, Eddie Waxer, of the International Sports Coalition Partnership based in the USA, told a meeting of the Forum of Bible Agencies in Colorado Springs that he got the vision for his global ministry from the example of the NBSS at the 1986 Commonwealth Games.

The NBSS, with the support of other Bible publishers, persuaded the major churches in Scotland to mark 1988 as the Year of the Bible. One of the many special events was the series of Prom Praise concerts, in major public venues across the country, which celebrated God's gift of his Word and raised new support for Bible work in different parts of the world.

A couple of years previously, during a family holiday in London, Dolina and I took the children to see the small Bible exhibition of the British and Foreign Bible Society. The children's reaction? 'Why don't you have a Bible exhibition in Scotland?' In 1991 Bibleworld was opened by the Queen, and five years later Bibleworld II was opened by the Princess Royal. Bibleworld I is Edinburgh based, while Bibleworld II is mobile, travelling to schools all over Scotland. Both deliver a hands-on, discovery-based learning experience. The lo-tech activities, like dressing up as monks and copying Scriptures in a medieval scriptorium, proved to be equally attractive to the children as the hi-tech work-stations.

While General Secretary in Scotland I became active in international work, visiting many countries which were short of Scriptures and meeting their church leaders. I will always remember in my first foreign trip, Peter Hatendi, Anglican bishop of Harare, telling me 'In Africa we have a crocodile appetite for Bibles!' Another unforgettable highlight was helping to lay the foundation stone of the Amity printing press in Nanjing, which has produced over 35 million Bibles and has helped so much to alleviate the urgent need for Scriptures in China's growing churches.

A global perspective
I was elected to serve on the United Bible Societies Regional Committee for Europe and the Middle East and, later, on the

global Executive Committee. The rapid growth of churches in the 'south' meant that Bible Societies were constantly straining their resources to meet the growing demand for Scriptures. I have always felt enormously privileged to be the ambassador of the many new Christians without a Bible when speaking in churches up and down Scotland.

During my years with the NBSS, my international involvement took two other forms. In 1984, I was invited to join the Lausanne Committee for World Evangelization (LCWE), an invitation which I accepted with the full support of my Board. Then, in 1996, I was appointed Executive Chair of the Lausanne Committee. The LCWE was set up after the initial Lausanne Congress of 1974 to promote collaboration in world evangelization, and the Lausanne Covenant (formulated at the Congress) has become a basis enabling evangelicals all over the world to work together in proclaiming the gospel in word and deed. Lausanne opened a door for me into the network of mission agencies and missiologists whose great burden is to pray, plan and work for the fulfilment of the Great Commission. Through this network I made many lasting friendships with evangelicals of a truly catholic outlook.

In 1997, I was encouraged by many friends to apply for the vacant position of General Secretary of the United Bible Societies. The UBS is the global network of about 140 Bible Societies, and its General Secretary is the CEO of the service arms that facilitate inter-Bible Society co-operation. I began my service as UBS General Secretary on 1 January 1998, based in Reading, England. I was genuinely sorry to leave the NBSS, but I regarded the UBS task as the global extension of what I had been doing in Scotland for seventeen years. My first tasks within the UBS were to encourage trust, to help deepen the spirit of fellowship, and work towards a new sense of direction. Many things happened during my four years with UBS, only three of which I mention here.

First was the approval at Midrand of the UBS statement on *identity and ethos*. The need for such a statement arose out of the rapid growth of new Bible Societies both in the southern hemisphere and also in Eastern Europe following the independence of the countries composing the U.S.S.R.. It was developed over a period of wide and prolonged consultation with Bible Societies that was open and transparent, and helped to build and consolidate mutual trust between young and old societies.

The second event was *Operation 21*, a U.S. $60 million programme of advance in translation, publishing and distribution of the Holy Scriptures. This initiative enabled the Word of God, in the form of some 85 million print Scriptures and 12 million non-print Scriptures, to impact many more lives and bring new hope to many more communities. The Scripture portion *Book of Hope* for schools in Haiti, a portion sensitively offered to AIDS-victims in Africa, the provision of thirty-five new distribution vehicles in China, the publication of 219,000 new Children's Bibles in India's major languages, and the translation of Scriptures into various Arabic dialects in the Middle East are examples of the 400 special projects making up the O-21 programme.

And the third development was the focus on *Scripture engagement*. The cutting edge of Operation-21 was the promotion of personal and group engagement with the Scriptures by audiences receiving them. This focus was, of course, not new. But at Midrand the role of Bible Societies in Scripture engagement was explicitly spelt out as 'helping people interact with the Word of God', and Scripture

18

engagement was formally recognized as a core activity of a fully functioning Bible Society.

Retirement – a new beginning

The Midrand focus on Scripture engagement brings me to my principal retirement activity. Scripture engagement had fascinated me all through my Bible Society experience. This fascination grew over the years as I realized that so many Scriptures distributed remain unused – in the waste bin, the bedside drawer or the bookcase. Are there ways, I asked, in which the Scriptures could be published and presented that would encourage much greater engagement with the text by the user? Traditionally Bible Societies have assumed that the churches take care of such matters. Moreover, in Christian countries the story line of the Bible was on the whole widely known. But today the situation is very different. Church attendance is in free fall, and the majority of people know little of the Bible's message. In addition, one key audience – those now in their twenties and thirties, sometimes described as *Generation X* – are intensely suspicious of the church (and of institutions generally), yet they have great interest in 'spirituality.'

In the western world the problem is not that Scriptures don't reach audiences beyond the church. The Gideons' distribution in schools and hotels, and the creative marketing of Bible Societies and other agencies, ensure that they do. The problem is that those who receive the Scriptures often don't know what to do with them! What can Bible Societies and other Bible agencies do to help new recipients engage meaningfully with the Scriptures they receive? During the last twenty years and more the Bible Societies have been grappling with how best to answer this question. They are clear that they do not wish to stray into the interpretive task of the churches, so marginal helps containing doctrinal interpretation are not on offer. Instead, the focus is on helps that are two-fold in nature. First, those that extend the translation process by providing linguistic, cultural and historical information implicit in the text but unknown to modern users. Second, helps which are inherent in the nature of Scripture as *story*, and which invite readers to enter into the story and engage with it by asking questions of the text arising out of contemporary felt needs and values.

The fact that this new focus is still in its early stages with much experimentation and piloting still requiring to be done, persuaded me, as I contemplated retirement, to undertake post-graduate research in this area. My particular audience is young adults in their twenties, who have an interest in spirituality but little or no contact with the church or with the Scriptures. I choose some Old Testament Psalms whose robust devotional tone resonates with the rather irreverent spirituality of 'GenXers.' I invite groups of around six people to undertake a five-week meditative *Psalm Journey* in which they meditate on a specific psalm for ten minutes every day for a week, keeping a daily spiritual journal, and at the end of the week they meet together for group meditation on the text and for sharing together. So far the results are encouraging: all the participants say they enjoy the journey, they are remarkably open and frank in sharing their experience of the text, and most indicate that they are now more likely to meditate on other biblical texts.

I believe that today we have a window of opportunity to engage with the new surge of interest in spirituality, and that the psalms lend themselves to being used as a means to this end. Research undertaken in the University of Nottingham by David Hay indicates that three-quarters of the U.K.

population are likely to admit to having had a spiritual or religious experience – an increase of 60 percent between 1987 and 2000. In our post-modern world people tend to be much more spiritually sensitive than they have been for the past few generations. Many people today openly acknowledge that they are engaged in a spiritual quest for meaning and fulfilment. For some this quest may be pre-eminently self-serving, as, for example, among many exploring New Age therapy. But there are others who are deeply concerned to discover some spiritual *shalom*, not only for themselves, but also for others and for the physical environment. For them life is basically a spiritual journey, and I think that they might be encouraged to explore pilgrim psalms like the Song of Ascents (Ps. 120–134).

Reaching Generation X

It seems that the younger end of the Generation X age-band is increasingly searching for 'roots' in ancient traditions. Surely the historical psalms (for example Ps. 78) are tailor made for them, for they encourage us to find our human significance in what the Lord had done for us in creation and redemption. Another characteristic of Generation X is its consciousness of pain – physical and psychological – arising from such things as parental divorce, child abuse and the fear of AIDS. The robust language of the psalms, which find expression in the vocabulary of searching, questioning, complaining, protesting and arguing in the presence of God, should resonate with them – if only they knew the psalms existed and would read them. This encourages me in my research, and the challenge at the end of it will be to persuade Christians that the age group they find most difficult to engage with, might be reached through the Book of Psalms.

I also believe that the psalms are becoming more, not less, relevant. It is increasingly obvious that we live in a blame culture. People sue whenever they think they can enrich themselves at the expense of someone else. One category of the Psalms of Lament is the songs of the falsely accused. Surely in a blame culture such songs are becoming ever more relevant. Again, we live in a society that is characterized by a sense of homelessness. In such a homeless culture the Songs of Zion – which rejoice in the Lord's dwelling among his people – strongly resonate with those searching for spiritual meaning and enlightenment.

The protest movement is once again finding its voice in western society, speaking out against globalization, environmental pollution, media oppression, exploitation of the poor, etc. Such voices might respond positively to lament psalms that were birthed in protest to God at the prosperity of the wicked. In a sense, these psalmists were the first 'protestants'! And our culture is increasingly a rage culture. In *The Scotsman* on 27th January 2004, Gillian Bowditch referred to road rage, air rage, and work rage, and made the following observation. 'We have trolley rage, perpetrated by middle-class housewives; property rage, the preserve of gazumped yuppies, and web rage, the crime of choice for hi-tech geeks.' One answer to this rage syndrome can be found in the imprecatory psalms! For, contrary to popular opinion, these psalms, by calling on God to deal with our enemies, affirm the principle of non-violence. The point has been made by Bonhoeffer and others, that the cursing psalms enable us to ask God to deal with those we hate rather than violently assaulting them ourselves. These psalms offer an antidote, not a toxin, to religious fundamentalist hatred. I am convinced that the psalms are deeply relevant to today's culture, and that Christians can and should make greater use of them in outreach. If the first few years of my retirement produce a thesis that will stimulate thinking of how this Book of Psalms can be used to reach out to our post-modern world with the gospel they will have been very well spent.

My research is full time, so it occupies a large part of the 'free' time created by my retirement. This means that there is not as much 'spare time' as I would like to do the kind of things I had looked forward to doing more of in retirement, like spending more time with the grandchildren, gardening, writing, DIY and caravanning. Of course, in addition to the research programme, there are other opportunities for Christian service: occasional preaching, serving as an elder in my local church, working in church committees, writing notes for Scripture Union's *Encounter with God* series, and speaking for the Scottish Bible Society and at various conferences.

But my main 'burden' is to help tomorrow's leaders encounter the Word of God as a dynamic and life-transforming message. Two months before I retired, the Bible Society General Secretaries in Central America bade me farewell in San Jose, Costa Rica. In the course of the evening I shared my plans for retirement and my Bible Society brothers made some very kind speeches that deeply moved me. The words that I remember most clearly were those of Rupert Neblett, of Panama, who said 'Perhaps as you retire you are about to begin your life's work!' Retirement – a beginning? Hardly! A sequel? Certainly! And hopefully also a climax!

2

DAVID AND JOYCE MOFFETT

It happened in the small village of Chincha Alta in the Montana of Peru in 1969, but it was to have a profound effect on us, and eventually led to what is happening in our lives in 2004. It was our wedding. We had already travelled a long way to reach that event and we were to travel a long way together in the years ahead.

Joyce remembers her childhood
I grew up in the Paddington area of London, England, where I was raised in a very rough area of the city. My father went overseas during the Second World

War and my mother and I were left on our own. It was a lonely time, but the Lord used it as Mum was drawn into a women's meeting run by the London City Mission in Kensal Road. There she found love and friendship and soon began attending other meetings as well. I accompanied her to these meetings. As we sat under the ministry of the Word, we both came to know the Lord when I was aged just ten. Another result of those meetings was that I felt the call to missionary service after watching a slide presentation by a missionary working with lepers.

Over the years I was helped along in my Christian life, and in pursuing my missionary call, by the various London City Missionaries with whom I came in contact. On the way to reaching my goal, I worked at Muller Orphanages in Bristol as a nursery nurse, took a government course on child care, worked in an orphanage, and directed a secular youth club seeking to present the gospel to the needy teenagers who came along. To further prepare for missionary service I went to Mount Herman Missionary Training College for two years, then stayed on for a year to be in charge of housekeeping there.

Finally I felt the Lord was leading me to serve as a missionary in Peru with the Regions Beyond Missionary Union. But even then the road wasn't easy. As the leaders of the RBMU were concerned about my ability to learn Spanish, they sent me to Spain to study the language at a university there. However, shortly after my arrival, I broke my leg and was laid up for the rest of my six months there. I did not learn much language, and there was very little opportunity to use what I did know as I lived with an American couple who spoke English. Finally the call came from Peru that the Mission was establishing a youth hostel for secondary schoolgirls in the main town of Tarapoto and it was felt that

I could be used in that ministry. So in June 1965, I set out for Peru, travelling first to Holland where I boarded a cargo boat for the three week long journey.

David's early years

I grew up in St Johnsbury, Vermont in the U.S.A. A religious boy who attended church whenever I could, even as a young lad, I sensed early in my life that God wanted me to be a missionary. By the age of ten I had been baptized and was a member of a Baptist church. However, although I thought I was a Christian, I was not. In May of 1950, when I was eleven years old, I attended a youth rally in a nearby town, and it was there that I heard the gospel afresh. That night I responded to the invitation and received Christ as my Saviour. After becoming a Christian, I realized that God was calling me to missionary service.

Having felt that call, I wondered where God wanted me to serve him. I considered both Africa and Europe, but in my first year of secondary school, I heard Rachel Saint speaking. She was then serving as a missionary in Peru. In her talk she said of the Indians with whom she worked that 'They live to die.' The phrase suggested such hopelessness and rang in my mind over the next few months until, that summer, I realized that God was calling me to Peru. In order to prepare for that calling I studied Spanish in secondary school and enrolled at Columbia Bible College in Columbia, South Carolina. After four years studying there, during which time I worked with Spanish-speaking soldiers at Fort Jackson and did another year of Spanish studies, I felt ready to go to Peru. But the Lord had other plans for me.

Immediately after graduation, he led me to Brooklyn, New York, to work with Spanish-speaking people and churches. During that time I applied to the Regions Beyond

Missionary Union and was accepted as a candidate. The following summer I went to Candidate School assuming that would lead to acceptance and then my going out to Peru. But I was wrong again. Because the Board still felt that I wasn't ready, they enrolled me in a programme called Missionary Internship, which involved me working with a church under a pastor. Nine months later, the Board felt there were areas of my experience that still needed development and they sent me to work with Open Air Campaigners in Newark, New Jersey. Finally in August 1964, I set out on a twelve-passenger freighter ship for the two week-long journey to Peru.

When I arrived I was able to get involved right away in the work because my knowledge of Spanish was sufficiently advanced. I was assigned to work with Fred and Ruth Webb, in the town of Chincha Alta on the Huallaga River. Ruth was a nurse and had a medical clinic while Fred had a ministry to the churches along the Huallaga, visiting them by boat and by motorcycle. My job was to help Fred with his ministry. During my time with the Webbs I accompanied them on a visit to one of the more isolated areas along a tributary of the Huallaga, the Ponasa.

Joyce tells how she and David met
It was about a year after David that I arrived in Peru to work at the hostel for secondary school girls. Shortly after my arrival, I accompanied other missionaries to a Church Convention in the town of Tabalosas. It was on this journey that I first met David. It was definitely not love at first sight. The journey took several hours by foot and horseback, but no romantic sparks were struck along the way. David remained in Tabalosas to help with the one hundred new converts who came to the Lord during the

Convention, while I returned to Tarapoto to prepare for the opening of the hostel in April. After a year working in the hostel, and trying to learn Spanish while doing so, it was decided that I should go to language school in Bolivia for more intensive language training. I did that, then returned to Peru where I worked in the hostel once again before being assigned to work in the Huallaga River area while Fred and Ruth Webb went home on furlough. Instead of continuing in Chincha Alta, where there was already an established church with its own leaders, I settled in the nearby town of Pucacaca. This was a larger town, and one that for many years had resisted the gospel. As a result of the move, and the work the Lord allowed me to do in Pucacaca, a church was established there. It continued after our marriage in the house in which we lived, and it is still going on today.

David tells what happened next
Meanwhile I had moved on to other ministries. After being in Tabalosas, I went with another single male missionary to the Cainarachi River area to help establish the work there. Following that I spent a time in Juanjui in the Upper Huallaga River area. Over the years since Joyce's arrival our paths had crossed, and because we were the only single missionaries of about the same age, some of our colleagues had inevitably linked our names. While they may have been trying to be helpful, that made it difficult for any relationship to develop. Finally, in 1968, I plucked up the courage to write to Joyce and express my feelings for her. From the correspondence that developed, we both began to realize that God was indeed leading us to join our lives together. So on 14th February 1969 we were married in that little town of Chincha Alta in Peru.

For the next nine and a half years we continued to serve the Lord in Peru, and during that time our three sons were born: Tim in 1970, Andrew in 1974, and Mark in 1976. In 1978, due to difficult circumstances, we felt the Lord leading us out of Peru, and we settled our family in Florida, U.S.A. where I worked at a Christian Radio Station and Joyce worked at a Christian School. In the summer of 1986 we spent three weeks in Guatemala working with the missionaries of the United World Mission. As a result of this summer trip, we sensed again the Lord leading us back to the mission field, this time to Venezuela with the United World Mission. After being accepted by the Mission, and raising financial support, we went to Venezuela in 1989, and spent six years there. I taught in the Bible school, training Venezuelan pastors, and Joyce was involved in the forming of ten children's clubs called Awana Clubs. We hosted several work groups from the U.S. who helped with buildings at the Bible School, and I also preached in many of the churches in the area. Once again the Lord used circumstances to show us when to leave Venezuela and he led us back to Florida.

Joyce remembers Florida
In Florida I got a job in another Christian School before going on to work for an organization called Healthy Families. That involved visiting pregnant women and following through with their children until they reached the age of five. Although working with a secular organization, and though not able to initiate conversations about God, I found that I was able to bear witness to the Lord in various ways. David, after several temporary jobs, secured employment in an insurance company working in the flood department and the mail room.

In 2001, on a visit to England, we were introduced to the London City Mission's Urban Track Programme through the Span Magazine. As we considered this opportunity for retirees to give a year working with the London City Mission, we felt that this was something that God would have us do. After all, retirement was just around the corner and we did not want to spend it sitting on rocking chairs. As long as the Lord gives us health and strength we want to use it for him. Not only that, it would be a way of saying thank you to the London City Mission for the input that they had in my life. After much prayer, and a further visit to London to meet with Harry Valance of the London City Mission, it was agreed that we would serve with them for a year. On 2nd January 2004, we retired from our secular jobs in the States, and one week later we flew to England to begin our year with the LCM. The Mission provided us with a house in the Downham area of Bromley, and assigned us to work in two different Mission Centres: Whitefoot Christian Centre in Downham and Malham Christian Centre in Forest Hill.

David describes the impact!
What a change from sunny Florida to winter in London! But that was just one of many changes we faced. Even Joyce felt it strange, and she is a Londoner! Although we had visited London over the years it was forty years since she had lived there. Not only that, but Joyce had been raised in the West End of London, now we were assigned to work in the Southeast of the city, in Kent. Interestingly, one of the London City Mission couples who had helped Joyce as a teenager and a young woman had actually worked in Bromley at the Downham Christian Centre not too far from where we were placed.

Joyce describes the changes she saw

A lot has changed in London since I left to go to Peru forty years ago. Today even the poor seem to have more. There are changes too in the church services, such as the use of overhead projectors instead of hymn books, and the use of many new hymns. Services have become much less formal and how people dress for church is much less formal too. Outstanding among the changes is the fact that London is more international. Sometimes I feel like asking 'Where did all the original Londoners go?' Another difference is the huge number of fast food restaurants and the big choice of ethnic foods. There are a lot more cars, and many people now take holidays abroad who would never have considered that possible when I was young in London. Educationally, greater numbers of children wear school uniforms, more pre-school services are offered, and there is a big increase in the number of children who attend private schools, and in the number of schools for them to choose from. One of the saddest changes that I have seen is the increase in homeless people living on the streets of London.

David recalls the early days

It took a while to settle in and get used to things, but we were soon involved in the work of the two Centres to which we were assigned. I was sent to Whitefoot Christian Centre while Joyce was to work at Malham Christian Centre on Mondays, Tuesdays and Friday mornings as well as helping out at Whitefoot on Sunday mornings and Thursdays. Our schedules are varied and sometimes we feel busier than when we worked in our secular jobs.

One of the things that thrills me is the privilege of preaching about one Sunday a month at Whitefoot. Added to that is the opportunity to teach a Bible study on Wednesday nights. But there is more to do at Whitefoot than that. Mondays are spent in staff meetings with the other workers at the Centre, and delivering free gospel newspapers, as well as doing door-to-door visitation in the area. Tuesdays are busy with a coffee morning, men's snooker club and children's club. The men's snooker club was especially interesting for me, as I had never played snooker before. It was a real learning experience! It is also a great opportunity to get to know the men and see what God is doing in some of their lives. Although asked to give a short talk at the coffee morning from time to time, my role is mainly to use opportunities to share in the lives of those who come for this time of fellowship, and to encourage them from the Word of God.

Two other opportunities for service at Whitefoot are the children's and youth clubs on Tuesday and Thursday afternoons. At the children's club – it's called Adventurers – I help maintain order and assist with different activities such as crafts and playing games with the children. They are a lively crowd as they come right from school. They seem to want to release some of the pent-up energy retained during their hours at school. The club allows them to receive teaching from God's Word and to learn Christian songs and choruses. At the Thursday youth club my role is as a helper, but there have been opportunities to share my testimony and to give short talks about God's Word. One of the exciting things is seeing the young people, who can be quite rowdy, sitting and listening to the Word of God as it is presented to them. All those involved in running the Club would love to see more evidence that the Word is provoking a response, but God, who knows their hearts, is able to move in them. He knows how much the Word is working in their lives. Also on Thursdays, I do some pastoral visits with Missionary

Paul Holland. This gives me the opportunity to work with someone who is able to communicate well on a one-to-one basis the truths of the gospel. I am privileged to participate in that communication.

Joyce describes her work

My ministry at Malham Christian Centre includes working with the Moms and Tots on Mondays and Fridays. This meeting is called The Rocking Horse Club, and it has brought in moms and tots from various national and cultural backgrounds. While the toddlers play, there is opportunity to talk with the moms, and while sharing their concerns we hope to share the gospel as well. There are other opportunities to serve and share as well, from making cups of tea to preparing teaching materials, to doing crafts with the children, to door-to-door visitation. While on visitation I met an older woman who was very depressed. This lady was unable to get out much and had very few contacts to brighten her day. I try to visit her once a week. We have a real rapport and God has given me the opportunity to share the gospel with her.

On Tuesdays, there is a staff meeting with those working at Malham and a fellowship hour with a Bible study, which each of the staff takes part in leading. Every third week there is a luncheon with a speaker and an opportunity to chat and share in a personal way. This involves food preparation and serving, plus cups of tea, and I help with that. I have also had the privilege of giving the talk at the luncheon. There are other duties in which I have become involved, including door-to-door visitation, which is the mainstay of London City Mission's work. On Thursdays, I help out at Whitefoot in the Moms and Tots. That's called Toy Time. The group there is smaller than at Malham, but again includes people from various cultural backgrounds. It also provides the opportunity to chat with the moms and a chance to share the gospel. In the afternoons, I help with the Youth Club and I have given the talk on one occasion.

On Sundays I attend the Sunday morning service at Whitefoot Lane, and from time to time give the children's story. I have told the story of the life of Amy Carmichael with flash card pictures. Adults as well as children seemed to enjoy that. Using her life story allowed me to present many truths about the Christian life. Once a month also I help serving coffee after the morning service, and help prepare for the Communion.

David tells us about their family
Our oldest son, Tim, is a Southern Baptist pastor in Panama City, Florida. He is married and has two children: Adam, who is nine, and Ashley, who is six. His wife, Susan is the daughter and granddaughter of Southern Baptist pastors. When we first decided to come with the London City Mission, Tim was a bit sceptical. Because I was preaching at the evening services in our church in St Petersburg, and teaching an adult Sunday school class, he thought I had plenty of opportunity to serve the Lord. However, when he realized that we truly felt this was what the Lord wanted us to do, he became very supportive of us in our venture.

Our second son, Andrew is a missionary with the Southern Baptists in Bolivia, South America. He is still single and has a great ministry of church planting in the city of Santa Cruz. Our youngest son Mark, works in an insurance company in St Petersburg, Florida, and is very active in our home church, especially with the young people. Both Andrew and Mark have also been supportive of us, and came over to visit in March.

It is wonderful how the Lord has led us from our wedding in Peru, to this present opportunity to serve him in the great city of London. We have just signed on for a second year with the London City Mission! And it will not end here, for the same Lord will lead us into the future until that final Retirement to Glory. Even then we will serve him in heaven.

3.

Beryl Gravelling

I was born in Cromer in 1927, having one sister then, and later another sister and brother. Junior school was a mile away. Most days we walked there and back, even at lunchtime, though sometimes Dad took one of us on his bike. At eleven years of age, I moved to a grammar school nine miles away in North Walsham, and I went there by train. We had a good education including many physical activities. That physical aspect of education, and playing a great deal of tennis at home, helped prepare me for my future career as a physiotherapist.

Our home was quite near a branch of the Overstrand Church, later Cromer Church. We attended there every Sunday along with many other children and their parents. Church clubs that met during the week gave us fun and sound Christian teaching. Like all the other children we knew, we were baptized and later confirmed. When I became a Christian many years later, I recognized the sound Biblical teaching we had had as children, and how that teaching was applied to moral standards and decent behaviour.

Whilst I was in the sixth form at school, a lady who was friendly with my aunt heard me speak my thoughts about my future career. I had an interest in pursuing a caring profession, but not necessarily nursing; and I loved sport. She told me of the five-year training at the Robert Jones and Agnes Hunt Hospital at Oswestry. Two years were spent training as an orthopaedic nurse, and three years as a physiotherapist. Most of the salary from the nursing years could be used to cover the physiotherapy training. I was very taken with the idea of this course as it meant I could train at no cost to my parents. An additional attraction was that the hospital was in the country, miles away from any bombing. This was, of course, during the Second World War.

Come now!
After one year in the sixth form I had a telephone call from the hospital asking if I would go a year early, as they had so many injured soldiers they needed more staff to care for them. So at the age of seventeen years and one month I went off to Oswestry. It was very hard work, and I had so much to learn, but because I was with so many other young people it was great fun. There were many new experiences to be met, among them the considerable disabilities and suffering I saw

in both adults and children. Young and old were confined to bed for months at a time. There were no antibiotics or other medicinal helps that we now take for granted, but my friends and I coped with all this without too many problems. Sadly, towards the end of my training, a beastly typhoid epidemic swept the hospital and many patients and staff, including myself, became seriously ill. A large number died, as there were no drugs to kill the bug. Unfortunately I developed a nasty complication of a pelvic thrombus that affected the circulation to my left leg. This caused me problems later in life. However, in spite of several months off sick, I managed to return to study. And when I took my final exams I passed them, thankfully.

I worked as a junior physiotherapist in a number of places including Norfolk, Oxford, Birmingham and Stoke Mandeville. During these years I had no real thought of Christianity. I guess I went to carol services but not much else. It was when I was working at Stoke Mandeville Hospital in the early 1960s that things changed. On arrival there some physiotherapists invited me to their Bible study group. I declined their offer quite strongly. A few months later I went to visit my brother John, who had qualified as a civil engineer and was working in London. I stayed in his digs and noticed a number of things with interest. The bedroom I used had Scripture verses on the mantelpiece. How odd, I thought, as I looked around. The doctor whose room it was seemed normal in other respects as there was a tennis racket and cricket bat in the corner. John and I did some interesting things, like going to Petticoat Lane and to a concert. Then on Sunday evening he said he was going to church, and asked if I would like to go with him. You could have knocked me over with a feather!

Westminster Chapel

On the way to church, John asked if I was a Christian. I thought that was a really strange question, and I do not know how I replied. We went to Westminster Chapel, and to my amazement the building was packed, and there was a large number of young people there. I went into church confident that I was OK, and that there was a place in heaven for me. After all, I was baptized and confirmed. Not only that, I had a good caring job and I was happy. What more did I want or need? The preacher, Dr Martyn Lloyd Jones, spoke for the best part of an hour, and when I left the church I knew that I was not OK, and I had no assurance of going to heaven. After the service John took me to the Antioch Club. This group met in the Westminster home of a Christian who held open house. It was not under the umbrella of Westminster Chapel. But it happened at that time that those who attended the Antioch Club also attended the Chapel, and they were all young. I was not there long before I realized that there was something different about them. What have they got that I don't have? I remember thinking:Whatever IT was I wanted it. In the weeks that followed reality hit me and, when the truth of the gospel dawned, I accepted Christ into my life. On returning to the hospital I informed the Christian physiotherapists that I wanted to join their Bible study group. They were overjoyed, and told me that they had been praying for me for six months. 'I will extol the LORD at all times; his praise will always be on my lips. My soul will boast in the LORD; let the afflicted hear and rejoice. Glorify the LORD with me; let us exalt his name together' (Ps. 34:1-3).

While working at Stoke Mandeville Hospital, I pondered the direction of my future career. The possibilities were to become a superintendent in charge of a department or to teach in a physiotherapy school. Having decided to pursue the latter, I applied to my old training school to do the appropriate course. Student life there had been enjoyable, and I looked forward to going back. Happy and rewarding describes my years at Stoke Mandeville, and successful too, as I was promoted. I had made many new friends and received enormous encouragement from Sir Ludwig Guttman, the doctor in charge. But when I went back to Robert Jones and Agnes Hunt Hospital at Oswestry things were different. I had no friends and discouragement seemed to come from every direction. Not only that, but because I was a student teacher I was effectively demoted. I had no one with whom to share my thoughts and concerns, and as a new Christian I found myself having to rely on the Lord completely. God became my friend and listener. I searched for an appropriate church, but none came up to my expectations. When I visited the local vicar seeking counsel and help, all he offered me was the Lord's Prayer. The lesson I learned from that experience was to listen to people and empathize with them, and to pray appropriately. I certainly gained some profitable, though hard, experience in a short time when I was a new Christian. 'The righteous cry out, and the LORD hears them; he delivers them from all their troubles. The LORD is near to the broken-hearted and he saves those who are crushed in spirit. The righteous man may have many troubles, but the LORD delivers him from them all ...' (Ps. 34:17-19).

God was good, and I finished my teacher training and gained the diploma required to teach physiotherapy. Soon after that, two people invited me to apply for the Superintendent post at the Norfolk and Norwich Hospital. About this time Sir Ludwig Guttman also invited me to apply for the same post at Stoke Mandeville Hospital when it became vacant. I prayed earnestly that God would direct

me and show me what to do. I applied for the Norfolk and
Norwich job, and at the interview I was completely truthful
about the situation. The interviewers told me that they
would quite understand if I went to Norwich then applied
for the other job when it was eventually advertised. But God
knew what the future held, and I remained in the Norfolk
and Norwich Hospital.

Answers to prayer

When I arrived there in 1965 I found the department run
down, with ancient equipment and very few staff. The morale
was low and there was no post-graduate training. Work was
done mostly for outpatients; very little was carried on in the
wards. In order to assess the needs I worked on different
wards in the hospital. When I was in an orthopaedic ward
one day I spotted a Bible on a man's locker. 'That's a good
book you've got there,' I said. He asked me my prayer needs.
'Please pray that God will bring some Christian staff,' I told
him. Within a short time a physiotherapist who attended the
same church as me asked if I could give her a part-time job.
Gradually the staff numbers increased and morale began
to rise. Soon after my appointment plans had to be made
for a new department that opened in 1971. Contacts with
physiotherapy schools facilitated further applications to the
point that we eventually had a waiting list! Post-graduate
training was implemented, and newly qualified staff rotated
round different departments and wards to gain experience.
In the early 1980s my responsibilities increased to include a
number of departments in different hospitals in the county,
and the commencement of a physiotherapy service in the
community.

Throughout the years there many decisions had to be
made regarding appointments; problems arose relating to

cost, working hours, patient coverage, quality of practice, and so on. The need for God's wisdom was so important. I know I made many mistakes, but what a lot more there would have been had I made the decisions on my own. It is thrilling to look back over these years and see how God was at work. On one occasion, when treating a patient from Los Angeles (a doctor of literature who had fallen and broken her back), I noticed a Bible on her locker. Once again that was an introduction to further conversation. I mentioned to her that I knew Margaret Rood, a physiotherapist in Los Angeles, who had written about some progressive techniques for neurological patients. To my amazement the woman knew her! Subsequently I was invited to visit the University of Southern California to meet Margaret Rood, and also to visit a very progressive physiotherapy department in Vallejo, near San Francisco – all expenses paid!

On another occasion one of my staff had a sister who was very ill in hospital. I felt it right to visit her. The cot sides were up; she was asleep and looking very ill. I placed my hand on her and prayed silently for her healing. Two days later, her sister asked me what had happened when I visited, because the patient was now so well that she was sitting up on a chair! God had answered that prayer.

There was a time when I was treating a lady who had a broken neck with considerable neurological damage to the nerves of her body, such that there was virtually no controlled movement. I was endeavouring to make her mobile to prevent stiffness and unnecessary pain and discomfort. 'Will you do me a favour?' she asked, quite suddenly. 'Why, yes, of course,' I replied, only to hear her sad request that I would help her to take her life. I said I could not do that, and that I would help her to keep it. I prayed with that poor woman, and asked various church members to pray that she would find a purpose to live. Months later I visited her at home. She was smiling from ear to ear. Although she was still paralysed, her husband had adapted many things at home in order to make life as easy as possible. 'My word,' I said, 'you look so much better.' Her reply was, 'Do you remember the day when I wanted to die? Well, that was the day my life changed.' Although there was no physical recovery, she had found a purpose to live.

One other patient I would like to mention was a man who was dying of cancer of the spine and had spastic paralysis of the legs. I was trying to make him comfortable when I noticed the terrible anxiety on his face. 'Are you worried about the future?' I asked. 'Yes,' he said, 'terribly.' My response was, 'If you can put yourself into the hands of God and let him carry you through, he will stay with you and give you peace.' That dear man began to smile and looked peaceful. I went to visit him the next day, but he had gone. I believe him to be with the Lord.

Looking back

When I retired in 1987, I was able to look back on my working life with great satisfaction and joy at the memory of how God worked in and through it. I'd had many Christian members of staff in my department. God certainly heard and answered my early patient's prayer. A number have been, and still are, serving missionaries. Two or three have been ordained and are serving God in different ways. There is so much for which I praise him. 'I sought the LORD, and he answered me: he delivered me from all my fears. Those who look to him are radiant; their faces are never covered with shame. This poor man called, and the LORD heard him; he saved him out of all his troubles. The angel of the

LORD encamps around those who fear him, and he delivers them' (Ps. 34:4-7).

On a personal note, I was a member of Holy Trinity Church, Norwich, where I had so much wonderful teaching from the clergy and others. And those who attended a Bible study group with me were supportive and long-lasting friends. In the mid 1970s, I realized one day that I was finding it difficult to walk, and I knew that the problem went back to my bout of typhoid. I saw the general surgeon who, following various investigations, decided that I needed urgent surgery on the deep veins. It was not easy to lay aside the busyness and responsibility of my job, even for a few weeks, but I knew it had to be done. There were also worries of further thromboses and embolism. I thank God that he brought Psalm 34 to my mind at the time. 'I sought the LORD, and he answered me; he delivered me from all my fears' (Ps. 34:4). With such a direct word from the Lord, I was no longer afraid. The day after my operation the surgeon told me that my leg would never heal, but it did.

Whenever I could, I attended Major William Batt's Bible study on Saturday afternoons in North Norfolk. Major Batt was an enthusiastic evangelist who was often away on missions. When he first invited me to join one of his mission teams, I asked how I could best prepare. 'You will probably be invited to speak at women's meetings,' he said. I didn't think that would be too difficult. But on being briefed during a mission at Weymouth I discovered to my amazement that I was the speaker the next day in Weymouth Church. 'Don't worry,' said the Major. 'God will tell you what to say.' And he did. It was also a great privilege over the years to work with Pathfinders whenever I could. This organization is superb at teaching youngsters the way of the Lord. And what fun it was to join them at camp on the Isle of Wight!

A new opening

Retirement, when it came, might have started with an empty diary, but it did not. The vicar of Holy Trinity Church, Rev. Keith White, invited me to serve the congregation as a pastoral care worker. This entailed visiting members of the church who were unwell or who had problems, also visiting homes for the elderly and taking services in them. I had a lot to learn, for my professional work had been mostly physical and I had little experience of social, moral or psychological problems. In visiting the elderly I recognized the terrible problem of loneliness. These dear folk needed encouragement to acknowledge that Jesus would never leave them. How important it was to visit regularly and to show God's love.

I met people suffering from a wide range of problems. For example, one evening I was called to the hospital where a beautiful young girl had asked for help from the church. She had nowhere to go and needed much help. This girl began to attend church fairly regularly. One evening I noticed her leaving church with my handbag. The vicar (in his robes!) and I ran after her and retrieved the bag. I hope that she recognized that we forgave her. I think she must have done, because some time later she asked me to go to the police station with her as she had a summons to appear there immediately. I promised I would stay with her. Little did I realize that she would be held in custody until a solicitor arrived. For the first time I found myself in a prison cell, where her fingerprints etc. were taken. I subsequently went to court with the girl. I don't know the outcome of her life, but I hope she recognized a touch of the love of the Lord Jesus.

One alcoholic first came to our church because he thumbed a lift from a lovely Christian man. He regularly visited our church, and eventually became a Christian. A number of church members supported him in as many ways as possible. One day I was driving into the city when I saw him entering a public house. Stopping immediately – on a double yellow line – I asked the publican to retrieve the bottle of vodka from the man and give him his money back. I then took him home in the car. God protected me from a parking fine on that occasion.

About three years into my retirement I moved to my home town of Cromer, where I purchased a lovely semi-detached house that I felt the Lord provided. It was dedicated to his use. Within a short time the vicar, Rev. David Haydn, invited me to be a pastoral worker for the area where I lived. He encouraged me to take a Bible study group, and I gladly accepted his invitation. The group started with one man and gradually increased to between ten and twelve, mostly retired people. We usually work through a book, and everyone is encouraged to take part and to join in our time of prayer. I am confident to say that all have come to faith and have grown in the knowledge and love of God, and some members who were not certain of eternal life now have assurance.

In Cromer my pastoral visiting again includes nursing homes and visiting those who are housebound, but I have became involved in other things too. Our church works with Faith in Action, a splendid Christian service that aims to help those in need in different places. Clothing, bedding, stationery and hospital items are among the things gifted. These are carefully prepared, packed into plastic bags, labelled, and then put into boxes to be shipped out to Rwanda. It is extremely rewarding to be involved in this work.

Where do I start?

Not long after moving to Cromer, I was invited to visit Arad in Romania to give advice on physiotherapy. This invitation came soon after the revolution. My brother had previously gone there with a van full of essentials, including Bibles that were much in demand. It was heartbreaking to see the very inadequate hospital services. Physiotherapy and rehabilitation were virtually non-existent, and many people suffered terribly as a result. It was difficult to know where to start, and I decided that I should teach nurses and carers simple rehabilitation methods. The staff were very keen to learn, and were somewhat amazed when I stood a lady on her feet, who had never stood before. She was about thirty years of age. The church I attended there was packed with young men who queued to get into the services. In their years of suffering the people had learned to depend on God. What a lesson to us.

Many people, knowing my professional background, ask for help regarding their physical problems. I always explain that I cannot treat them but that I am happy to give advice. Muriel, a member of our congregation, suggested that we have a 'look after yourself' class. She would take exercises to music and I would give specific exercises for posture, breathing, relaxation and care of certain joints. Whilst practising relaxation, Muriel suggested that we have a verse from the Bible and a short prayer, and the group went along with this. When I started I had no thought of a spiritual dimension to the class, but God has used these gatherings to his glory. We call ourselves SWELS, Seniors with Energetic Lifestyles. One lady progressed from SWELS to an ALPHA course where her faith developed, and she is now working hard for the Lord.

As I look back on my life since I became a Christian in the 1960s, I praise and thank God for so much. I thank him for my brother John, who took me to hear Dr Martyn Lloyd Jones and led me to God. I praise the Lord for the love, support, teaching and fellowship of fellow Christians and leaders in the church. And most of all I thank the Lord with all my heart for the wisdom, guidance and love I have known through his Holy Spirit. Retirement so far has been full, interesting and varied; and with God's help I hope to serve him for the rest of my life on earth. 'Taste and see that the LORD is good; blessed is the man who takes refuge in him. Fear the LORD, you his saints, for those who fear him lack nothing. The lions may grow weak and hungry, but those who seek the LORD lack no good thing' (Ps. 34:8-10).

4.

JIM CROMARTY

My growing up days were spent on the family farm about twenty-five miles north of Newcastle, Australia. In many ways life there was exciting. We had our horses to ride, dogs and cats for pets and even a nanny goat. I can't remember how we came to own a goat, but I do remember that she frequently ate the daily newspaper if it was thrown too close to her by the mailman, who not only delivered the mail, but many small items from Raymond Terrace, our nearest town. A replacement newspaper meant a ride on our bikes to Raymond Terrace to get a second copy. I can remember the first car Mum and Dad owned – a T Model Ford. This was followed by one of Australia's home made Holdens. When we were very young it was the horse drawn sulky that took us about. Grandfather, who was totally deaf, used to visit his relatives about thirty miles away. My brother John and I frequently accompanied him in the sulky to have a couple of days with our cousins. But it was a long trip for two energetic boys.

I can still remember the man who delivered huge blocks of ice for our ice chest. Later, when my parents purchased an electric refrigerator, Mum made ice cream, which we all enjoyed. Living on a farm meant there was always food on the table. The garden provided our vegetables, and occasionally an animal was slaughtered to add to our meat supply. We had chores to do, and as John and I grew up we decided that farm life was not for us. Both of us wanted to be school teachers. Farming meant too much work without a holiday. The cows had to be milked twice each day, and I can still remember hand milking them before we had electric milking machines. Often we were out of bed early to help Dad in the dairy. To keep warm on those cold frosty mornings, we rested our heads against the warm side of the cows as we milked them.

Messing about on the river

Our farm was close to a junction of two rivers, and we had a rowing boat, in which John and I spent many happy hours fishing. The rivers were frequently in flood, and we enjoyed swimming in the muddy floodwater. While we were happy because we couldn't get to school, our parents were distressed by their loss of crops. Only once did the flood get into our home, but many times the house was surrounded for a week or more by a sea of muddy water. I belonged to the Sea Scouts, and rode my bike the three miles to Raymond Terrace once each fortnight for the exciting times we had together there. Both John and I developed a love of classical music when we were eleven or twelve years old, and that love has continued. Today we both have our collections of operas and singing by the world's greatest operatic stars. We shared another great love, and that was The Goon Show. I can remember lying down on the floor of the lounge each Saturday night, laughing at the antics of Spike Milligan, Harry Secombe and the others!

Each weekday I rode my bike to the three-teacher primary school at Raymond Terrace, where I enjoyed the challenges of learning, especially reading widely and written expression. In the playground I was a competent marbles player – in fact, I can still beat my grandchildren! Several times I received the cane, but to this day I believe that the reason for this punishment was unfair! Secondary school was an all boys school in Maitland, about twenty miles distant. We travelled there by bus, and that meant an early morning start. Often we risked our lives by getting off the bus with some friends in order to swim in the river. We spent many hours, jumping off the bridge into the water, ten or fifteen feet below. In those days I was fit and a good swimmer. The journey home on the late bus was spent inventing excuses for our late arrival.

At Maitland High I detested learning French, but enjoyed writing and sport. I played in the second, and then the first grade rugby football team. They were good days! Each school vacation I worked at the Masonite Factory to earn some pocket money. Once again that meant heading off on the push-bike, as the factory was about two miles distant from Raymond Terrace. Each day I worked my eight-hour shift with the men and, like them, I always looked forward to pay day. Mum and Dad could not afford regular pocket money.

History of the PCEA

Our family attended worship in the Presbyterian Church of Eastern Australia (PCEA). In the days following the settlement of Australia by Europeans, there were many from Scotland who settled along the east coast. They brought their faith with them, and a few stood firm with the Free Church of Scotland when the Disruption took place in 1843. That was our church. Our family attended worship each Lord's Day but, as there was no Sunday School, we attended the one in the Methodist Church before going to our service. I went to church because I was told to do so! For some reason our family had no daily family devotions, nor did we attend church camps or learn the catechism. However, I still have my Bible (the Authorized Version) which I read for many years before and after my conversion. John and I were encouraged to read widely, no doubt partly because my mother was at one time the librarian of the Raymond Terrace Public Library. One wall of a bedroom in our home had shelving to the ceiling filled with books, including the six volumes of Matthew Henry's Commentary on the Bible, and many of Spurgeon's sermons.

My father's parents lived with us on the farm, and it was Grandfather who, shortly before his death, spoke to me about my standing before God. I listened closely to all he said. He had fallen ill, and for a month or so his health deteriorated until he knew death was close. Grandfather called me to his bedside and there told me of his love for Christ, and pressed upon me my need to repent of my sins and trust in the Lord Jesus for my salvation. Of course, more was said than that, but I was only twelve years old and it made such an impression on my mind that it remains with me today. I look forward to meeting him again in heaven.

Life changes

After secondary school I received a scholarship to attend Newcastle Teachers' College, where I met the sister of one of the boys who attended Maitland Boys High. It wasn't long before Val and I became very close friends. At that stage neither one of us was converted, but we both attended worship and read our Bibles. In fact, when Val won a College book prize, she asked for and received a Bible. When College days ended, Val was teaching in Maitland and I was posted to a one-teacher school about 600 miles away at Iron Pot Creek! To get there I travelled by train and with the postman. He transported me to the home of the family with whom I was to board for eighteen months. The man of the house was a convert to Roman Catholicism. When we met he asked me if I had a Protestant Bible with me. To my 'Yes', he told me he didn't want to see it anywhere in his home. It was this that made me turn to my Bible more than anything, as I had a reason to search the Scriptures and discover why he felt as strongly as he did.

It was in that home that I was introduced to Roman Catholicism. Each night the family met to recite the Rosary and the Lord's Prayer, while I remained in my room reading my Bible. The family faithfully kept the fast days – no meat on Friday – although the big, juicy steaks on Saturday more than made up for the fast. The family also fasted before going to church to celebrate Mass. One Sunday, one of their daughters, who was on the verandah fiddling with a pumpkin, suddenly gave a cry of distress. Running to her mother, she confessed that she had chewed and swallowed a pumpkin seed! The girl was not permitted to participate in the Mass that day because she had broken her fast. A Christian friend, who knew the circumstances in which I was living, told me to purchase Matthew Henry's Commentary, Calvin's Institutes, Archbishop

Ryle's Commentary on the Gospels and a systematic theology, and get to work prayerfully reading them. No small task!

I read the Bible as never before, and for some months became deeply convicted of my sins. It was at that time that I was transferred to another one-teacher school that was aptly named, Repentance Creek. I continued to read the Bible and the other books, but couldn't comprehend why salvation appeared to be so simple – how my sins could be placed upon Christ and how his righteousness could be put to my account. I couldn't grasp the doctrine of justification by faith alone. On 9th August 1958, while attending a Baptist Church crusade, the Lord opened my eyes to the salvation so freely available in the Lord Jesus. Everything fell into place! I remember the date, because I still have the small book I purchased: *Sacrifice: A Challenge to Christian Youth* by Howard Guinness, and I inscribed the date on the front page. In the meantime Val and I had announced our engagement, though it was a romance carried out by correspondence. Neither of us had a car, and we only saw one another during the school holidays. Immediately after our marriage, Val was surprised that I took my typewriter on our honeymoon. I thought I'd have time to do some writing. The typewriter was largely untouched!

Working years

We were both appointed to schools in the Sydney area where we regularly attended the local Baptist church. It was in 1959 that the Billy Graham Crusade visited Sydney and, with many people from the local churches, we attended the meetings. At one of those meetings Val saw her need of a Saviour, and turned to Jesus Christ as her only hope in time and eternity. Our love of books increased and over the years we built up a sound Christian library. As teachers we were transferred about New South Wales. I was appointed to Tilbuster, another one-teacher school, and the demonstration school attached to Armidale Teachers' College. Consequently, I regularly demonstrated the art of teaching to the College students though I was a student myself, having just completed my B.A. degree, and commenced work for a Master of Letters qualification. We attended the Presbyterian Church in Armidale.

When transferred to the position of Principal of Oxley Island, which was situated on an island in the Manning River delta, we rejoiced as a family, as at long last we could attend the Presbyterian Church of Eastern Australia. While living on Oxley Island I bought a boat that my brother and I used for fishing out on the ocean. There were exciting times – especially the morning the boat capsized about five hundred yards from the shore! But the Lord took care of us both. Soon after that John, who was the Deputy Principal of Maitland Primary School, resigned from teaching and commenced studies for the Christian ministry in the PCEA. Meanwhile, I was appointed the Deputy Principal of the town in which we had built our house. Our four daughters were growing both physically and spiritually, and for that we thank the Lord. We had family worship each morning as that was when we were all seated at the table together.

During those days I felt called to use my gifts in the ministry, and this was reinforced by encouragement from our minister, Rev. Edwin Lee and members of the congregation. When I was appointed the non-teaching principal of quite a large primary school nearby, our family settled down to a comfortable existence. However, after five years there, Val and I agreed that I should approach the appropriate body with the request that I enter the ministry of the PCEA. The Presbytery, and later Synod, decided that I should work in the Hunter River congregation, while the church ministers ensured that I was trained, including two years study of Greek at a local theological college. Before moving I sold my fishing boat in order to avoid the temptation to spend too much time fishing instead of doing the Lord's work.

Several years later I was ordained, and within a short time the Hunter River congregation, which I had attended as a child, gave me a call that I accepted instantly. Those days were some of the happiest Val and I have experienced. The Lord blessed the congregation and our numbers grew. But after about nine years, I injured my back and needed surgery. I expected everything would be back to normal again after the surgery, especially as a doctor told me I would be able to dig potatoes within a couple of months.

Another door opens
Things did not work out quite as I expected, and I spent the following months, tormented by pain and mental distress, wondering what the Lord was doing to me. My enforced incapacity did not only affect Val and me, but it impacted on my congregation too. They were special people to me, many were related and others I had known for years. One lady often enjoyed telling me how she had nursed me on her knee when I was a baby. Others had been converted during my ministry; that's how good the Lord had been to us. The questions that kept coming to my mind were: 'Why has the Lord done this to me? How can I be involved in the Christian ministry now?' But the question really was: what does someone in my physical state do who has been used to an active life?

Many years before, John and I had made an agreement that when we retired we would buy a boat for ocean fishing. We both thoroughly enjoyed fishing, and looked forward to the day when we'd spend our time out on the ocean swell pulling in the big ones. But that was not to be. My hope of fishing my life away did not materialize because the Lord had different plans for me. And since my surgery, pain and disability have given me a much better understanding of the teaching of Romans 8:28: 'And we know that in all things God works for the good of those who love him, who have been called according to his purpose.'

I remember Val telling me to take up tapestry, which I did, and found it very relaxing. But I saw it as a stopgap until I would get back to work. We were still living in the manse, and had no plans to move as I thought the Lord would heal me. However, our days there were soon to end. Our God is a God of grace, and the One who knows the future because he planned it. Before my illness, Val and I decided to build a house for the day I retired, or to have a house for her, in case I died. Then the day came when the doctor told me I would have to retire, as my health was not going to improve. We therefore moved to our home in Wingham much earlier than we had anticipated. Giving up the ministry and leaving the manse upset me greatly, but God gave Val the strength to arrange for our move.

We were no sooner settling into a different lifestyle than a life-threatening illness appeared. During the previous four years I had suffered regular kidney stones, but no one realized they were symptoms of a parathyroid tumour. With the tumour removed, I quickly recovered, although I was left needing more medical treatment. Life had again become very stressful. I found difficulty walking and suffered continual pain. A trip to a pain clinic resulted in me being prescribed morphine. That along with other medication, left me feeling very weary, but I continued with my tapestry.

It was then, when I wasn't really able to make major decisions for myself, that Val made two decisions of importance for me. She bought me a lovely little Maltese dog that was to be my 'pet therapy'. And Wags has been a good mate for the last nine years! He enjoys his morning walk, after Val and I conclude our morning devotions. As soon as Wags hears 'Amen' he commences barking. To him 'Amen' means walk! Val also suggested that I buy a computer and start writing. After all, hadn't I been so keen to write that I'd taken my typewriter on our honeymoon! We had never owned a computer, but we bought the 'user friendly' MacIntosh, and set to work producing a monthly paper for our church young people. At last I was writing and had all the time I needed to do it. For the first time since my back injury I felt very satisfied with what I was doing.

A new career

One day a pastor friend from Newcastle called in, accompanied by the late Mr Bill Clark from Evangelical Press, who showed a great deal of interest in my new computer and the children's magazine. He asked me to send him copies of some of my stories. However, I was still unwell, and neglected to mail them to him. About three months later he wrote, again asking me to please send him some samples of my stories for children. The first outcome was the seven Family Reading books which have, in all, three hundred and sixty-six stories with Scripture teaching. Then came biographies, one published by Christian Focus Publications: *It is not Death to Die*, which is a biography of Hudson Taylor. And Evangelical Press published *A Mighty Fortress is our God, King of the Cannibals, Food for Cannibals*, and *The Pigtail and Chopsticks Man*. Writing is not a solo work, and other people have been a great help to me. Val, a former school teacher, proved to be an excellent proofreader, as did Elizabeth, my sister-in-law, and Lindy Gadsby, our pastor's wife. They are the ones who keep me humble!

Still fishing!

As time passed and I saw my books published, it became clear to me that I was still of use in the Lord's service. I was still a fisherman. Just like Peter and his brother Andrew, I was fishing for souls. 'As Jesus was walking beside the Sea of Galilee, he saw two brothers, Simon called Peter and his brother Andrew. They were casting a net into the lake, for they were fishermen. "Come, follow me," Jesus said, "and I will make you fishers of men."' (Matt. 4:18-19). It is this fishing that really matters! The correspondence we have received from readers in many continents shows just how widely the net has been cast. At the end of each of the Family Reading books I have my name and address and a request for comments and a postcard from those who have read the book. We have hundreds of postcards now.

Several years ago Val and I visited the Christian Booksellers' Convention in Atlanta, in the U.S.A., as guests of Evangelical Press. There we met one of the families who had corresponded with us after reading the Family Reading series. They took us to worship in their church and then to their home where they had about thirty guests ready to hear about Australia and about my writing. We would never have made such a journey, except for the kindness of Evangelical Press. That trip showed me something special. It taught me that when God makes us fishers of men, the fishing line can go a very long distance indeed!

And now?

I turned down eldership in our congregation, as I'm of the opinion that a retired minister could make life uneasy for the pastor. However, I have my Bible Study/Prayer group; Val has the same with a group of ladies, and together we visit members of the congregation. The writing continues. In 2004, *A Year with your Children in the Bible* was published by Evangelical Press, as well as *Outback Adventures,* a children's book for Christian Focus Publications' Adventure series.

It is so hard to believe what has happened in my days of retirement. I now write books just as I had always longed to do. Not only that, but I have all the time I need and my congregation is now worldwide. Several books have been translated into Russian, and one into Romanian. These titles are now being used on the mission field. My brother John read my biography of Martin Luther on to tapes, and they are now available too. I haven't been fishing for years, and the boat is long gone, but through God's grace I'm still casting my line for him. The results are in his hands.

Even in weakness I am of use to the Lord, and for that I give him thanks. My talents come from God, as does my salvation. The words of Psalm 92 have been shown to be true in my own case, and they are a joy to sing:

Like palms and cedars flourishing
the righteous all will be,
And planted in the house of God,
will grow abundantly.

So in old age they still bear fruit;
they will stay fresh and strong.

They will proclaim: 'The Lord is just
my Rock, who does no wrong.'

5.

THOMAS H. BOWEN, JR

I am a Mississippi man. More specifically, I am a sixth generation Mississippian. Born in 1930 as the son of Thomas H. Bowen, Senior, and Carolyn Allen Bowen, I am someone who can trace his roots. The Bowen family has made Mississippi its home since the 1830s, when my maternal great-great grandfather first came to serve as a missionary. Visit a historic cemetery in Grenada County, and there you will find some of my ancestors. Research town records from the nineteenth century, and the family is prominently mentioned. Peruse the archives of local churches, and there you will find many of my relatives, active in their original organizations.

My mother could place her family in the area as far back as the late eighteenth century, when the land was still under Spanish control, years before the official organization of Mississippi as a state. And the ties don't end simply with the state of Mississippi. My mother, Carolyn, was a fifth generation resident of southwest Mississippi, and Port Gibson, a small town of about 2,000 residents, located near the banks of the Mississippi River, and the place that I think of as home. Though I moved from Port Gibson to Jackson for employment reasons more than forty years ago, Port Gibson can never be replaced in my heart. There's just too much history there.

Spiritual heritage

As important as my family's heritage is, and as deep as my roots stretch down into the red Mississippi clay, the most important family history deals not with my genealogy, but with the spiritual heritage passed down by my parents. For while I take great pride in my family name, and in the accomplishments of my ancestors, I have no doubt about their relative importance. You see, I grew up in a home where my father made it his habit to gather the family in the evenings for family worship, where the Bible was read, and where family prayers were recited. We frequently gathered around the piano, where Daddy would bang out the familiar tunes of much-loved hymns of the faith. It was there that I first began to learn about the Bible, and about the God revealed in Holy Scripture. It was there in the evenings that I saw the reverence our family had for God's Word, the sincerity of my parents' faith, and the reality of my own need of a Saviour. It was there that my parents, who made it their goal to bring up my sister Janis and me in the fear and admonition of the Lord, first sowed the seeds of faith. Though my father struggled with alcoholism for much of his fifty-two year life, I never doubted the man's commitment to the Lord. In fact, I am now, many years later, able to look back at some of the struggles and hardships created by my father's misuse of alcohol, and see how God has used those experiences to prepare me for work to be done later in life. And the godly example of my mother's efforts to hold the family together seared the lesson of dedicated service in my young, impressionable mind. This is the history I love to recite, and this is the history that I credit as foundational to my life.

I grew up attending the First Presbyterian Church of Port Gibson. As an active member in all facets of that congregation's activities, I was taught both at home and at church the truths about God, and the gracious gift of salvation found only in Jesus Christ. Like so many children of believing parents, my testimony begins with and rests upon the faithfulness of God. With credit to the witness of my parents, the solid instruction of the church, and ultimately, the sovereign grace of God, I came to a saving knowledge of the Lord at a very early age. I was received into communicant membership at First Presbyterian Church Port Gibson in 1940, at the age of nine.

My involvements in the church went beyond simple attendance. I was there for worship on Sunday, participating in the praise of my heavenly Father. I was involved in periodic conferences, summer camps, and Sunday school. And during my teen years, I served as the president of the Church League, a Sunday evening youth group. This high level of involvement in the local church has continued throughout my life. In 1958, I joined First Presbyterian Church in Jackson, Mississippi. Twenty-one years later, the congregation elected me as a deacon, an office I held for seven years. In 1986, I was elected as a ruling elder, and have continued in that capacity since then. I have been privileged to serve on a number of committees, and have been the Sunday school secretary/treasurer for nearly thirty years.

After graduation from Port Gibson High School, I attended Hinds Community College, where I met my future wife Betty McLendon. Before the end of my first year there, I was called into active service as part of the military's mobilization for the Korean War. Upon the completion of my active service, I enrolled in the Louisiana State University College of Commerce, where I earned a Bachelor of Science degree and Air Force Reserve Officer Training Course (ROTC) commission. My education also included a stop in New York, at the Stone and Webster of New York Executive Training School, and the National War College in Washington, D.C., for reserve officers.

Betty and I were married in 1951. God blessed our marriage with two daughters, Elizabeth Bowen Pollock and Mary Allen Bowen McBride. We now enjoy the blessings of five grandchildren.

Still in Mississippi

My professional career began with the Southern Bell Telephone Company, and I worked as a manager there for seven years. From Southern Bell, I moved to another utility company, finding a home at Mississippi Valley Gas Company. Beginning as an administrative assistant, I found the work rich and rewarding. I remained at Mississippi Valley for twenty-eight years. Labouring within the administrative office, I was able to work my way up to vice president of administrative services, overseeing all facets of human relations, including legal matters and risk insurance, before my retirement in 1994. I served Mississippi Valley as a member of its executive management committee, chief labour negotiator, equal employment officer, and occupational safety act officer. The Southern Gas Association also honoured me in 1985, when they elected me chairman of their annual convention.

Involvement in the Jackson community did not end with my employment at Mississippi Valley Gas Company. I was pleased to serve on several local and state commissions and boards, including the Hinds County Youth Court Advisory Board, the State Personnel Board, the Jackson Public Schools Trust Foundation, Leadership Jackson, and the Jackson Symphony. In addition, I was an active member of the Metro Jackson Chamber of Commerce, serving as its Chairman of the Education Committee, and a Paul Harris fellow with the Rotary Club. In what spare time I had, I enjoyed working as a historical tour guide for a variety of functions throughout southwest Mississippi.

In addition to the various roles God was gracious enough to allow me to enjoy in the private sector, only half of the story of my working life has been told. As well as my civilian service, I also served my country and the Department of Defence in some manner for more than fifty years. A veteran of both the Korean and Vietnam Wars, I served in the Air Force, Air Force Reserves, and Air National Guard for thirty years, retiring as a Colonel. Since then, I have continued to serve the Defence Department in a variety of functions, most notably as the Chairman of the Mississippi Committee for the U.S. Defence Department Employer Support for the Guard and Reserve National Committee. Indeed, including my honorary protocol rank, I have served in every military rank from Private to Major General, except three.

A tool in the hands of God

It is easy to see through this sampling of my civilian, civic, and military highlights, that God greatly blessed me, and allowed me to enjoy a rich and fulfilling professional career. My gifts and abilities were given to me by the Lord, and used by him to enable me to serve a variety of organizations. In turn, God blessed me with new and rewarding opportunities for service. Indeed, reflecting upon the many facets of my career, all I can say is that the successes were not of my doing. God graciously used me as a tool in his hands.

In 1994, after twenty-eight years of employment with Mississippi Valley Gas Company, and at the age of sixty-four, I retired. Of course, my retirement was never a complete retirement. I continued to function as an Admissions Liaison Officer for the Air Force Academy in Colorado, interviewing young men and women to help identify those worthy of acceptance to the Air Force Academy. In addition, I became more involved as a tour guide, being recognized as an authority on the Port Gibson and Grand Gulf campaigns of the United States War Between the States.

The lakeside idyll?

My wife and I had big plans for retirement. As I am somewhat of an avid hunter, and we both enjoy the peacefulness of the outdoors, we began making plans for a lakeside cabin on Lake Caroline. With free time to spare and renewed energy, we began to travel, most notably enjoying a trip to Europe. Yet God eventually demonstrated that he was not yet finished with me. The professional gifts and experience he had given me were to be called into service again, though this time not within a utility company. Before the fourth year of my retirement ended, a new employer came knocking on the door. Only this employer was not just looking for a decorated service man, or simply an experienced executive. This employer was in some trouble, and was looking for someone who could help save his organization from the brink of financial ruin. And as it turned out in God's providence, this new opportunity was one already close to my heart. I was needed by an institution deeply ingrained in the fabric and history of Port Gibson, Mississippi, and one deeply engulfed in financial and administrative difficulties. On the brink of closing its doors, the Chamberlain-Hunt Academy, the last remaining Christian military academy in Mississippi, Louisiana, or Arkansas, reached out to me for some help.

It was 1998, and the lakeside cabin that had previously only existed in our dreams had just been completed. A second trip to Europe with my wife was already being planned, and retirement was becoming a nice fit. Who would have known that a simple request for some advice on a business deal would end my retirement and lead me into a hornets' nest? Chamberlain-Hunt Academy had been a mainstay in Port Gibson since the late nineteenth century. Started by the Presbyterian Church as a distinctively Christian military school, it had enjoyed a long history of community support for its work, especially with troubled children and teenagers. Accepting students both from the community, but particularly as boarding students, it had a reputation as a sound academic facility, and a place where young people who needed the opportunity to learn and grow away from home could find structure, discipline, and people who cared.

Insolvent

Things had been declining at CHA for many years, to the point that it was on academic probation by the Mississippi

Private School Association. Bible instruction had been almost completely removed from the curriculum. Facilities were in disrepair, and it was becoming increasingly difficult to attract new boarding students, who were the financial backbone of the institution. As is often the case, the problems were snowballing (even in the hot Mississippi climate!) and CHA had become financially insolvent.

Holding nearly $1,000,000 in uncollectable notes, two local banks stepped in and took control of the property. They offered to pass ownership of the property and facilities to French Camp Academy, a Christian boarding school started by the Presbyterian Church in 1885, and located about 150 miles north of CHA. The French Camp Academy's Vice-President and a close friend of mine, Ed Williford, contacted me to ask for my advice on the proposal. But that original request for counsel turned into a request for personal involvement. After successful negotiations, and with an agreement in place for ownership of Chamberlain-Hunt Academy to be assumed by French Camp Academy, I was asked by the Board of Trustees at FCA to be Interim President at CHA.

I was shocked by the request. The Board of Trustees wanted me to serve for just three months, to provide some stability during the early phases of the transition. After touring the French Camp facilities, and receiving loud support from the community in Port Gibson and Chamberlain-Hunt (now officially known as Chamberlain-Hunt Academy, a ministry of French Camp Academy), I sensed God leading me into this new opportunity. Indeed, I could look back at the various experiences of my life and see how he had been preparing me for this unique and challenging position.

Adrift from its moorings

When I arrived at Chamberlain-Hunt in April of 1998, I was aware of the financial insolvency. But as I stepped on to the campus, what I found was far more trouble than the matter of unpaid bills. As a microcosm of the physical neglect the Academy had suffered, my living accommodation, the 'President's House', was without furniture and without a working air-conditioner. I found myself sleeping in the dormitory, enjoying the same arrangements as the cadets. The administration too suffered from a lack of vision and communication. Though much of the staff was committed to the work of CHA, a culture of mistrust and disunity had been allowed to develop, and the school had lost its distinctive Christian moorings. Enrolment by boarding students was dangerously low.

But what became apparent immediately was that this was no short-term job. How could I simply bide my time at the school for three months and then leave it still teetering on the edge of disaster? It was going to require a tremendous personal commitment to the school, and that commitment would need to last more than three short months. If I had been a quitter, I would have turned around for Jackson right then to continue enjoying my retirement in comfort and peace. But instead I decided to stay, and officially removed 'interim' from my title.

Though the task was daunting I found that God had been preparing me for this task, and that he was strengthening me for the charge. My experiences as a child of an alcoholic left an indelible impression upon me, and created a special place in my heart for any child growing up in a family that is fractured or in trouble. The involvement in the Hinds County Youth Court Advisory Board gave me a close-up and personal look at some of the difficulties faced by children from broken homes. Even my duties as a Liaison Officer for the Air Force Academy kept me working with young people. And of course my labours as the Sunday school secretary/treasurer at First Presbyterian Church allowed me to see the importance of biblical instruction in the lives of children. God had provided new and fresh opportunities to work with children and young adults throughout my life, and I needed all of that experience as I undertook my new role as president of CHA.

As my first priority, I set out to reintroduce the subject of the Bible back into the curriculum. When I arrived, only senior students were required to take a Bible class, and then only twice a week. Recognizing the central importance of proper biblical instruction for the health and well-being of CHA, we ensured that it became a daily subject for all cadets at the Academy. I also introduced a 'Team Concept of Management', employing the use of ten committees that worked together to further the corporate goals of CHA. Instead of competing departments working against one another, my vision was for all of them to pull in a collective direction. I placed a renewed emphasis on recruiting new boarding students, who had in many ways become secondary to the day students from the Port Gibson area. And I saw to it that the ethical standards of the students and staff reflected the motto: 'We do not lie, cheat, curse, steal, or tolerate anyone around us who does.'

Leaning on Everlasting Arms
But as is so often the case, change was not always met with open arms. There were those who were not happy with some of these new ideas. Some staffing changes had to be made, new policies introduced and implemented, and it all had to be done quickly. There were many hurdles, many close calls,

and many days of discouragement. Yet God was faithful to me and to CHA. Leaning on the Everlasting Arms, I was able to keep going.

Despite the opposition, the innovations were almost immediately successful. Through the generosity of French Camp Academy, structural improvements were made, updating the facilities to more liveable conditions. Leaking roofs were replaced. Air-conditioning units were installed. Computers were bought for the students, and a new computerized accounting system was introduced to help implement financial controls. The cafeteria was updated, with new, working appliances. Broken and worn-down furniture was renewed, and floors repaired. A more substantial one, appropriate to carry the nation's flag at a military academy, replaced even the diminutive flagpole. Boarding cadet enrolment increased to fifty students, up from twenty-two just the year before. New teachers were added, and curriculum changes made to return the quality of education to its previous high standards. Communication between the departments was greatly improved. And communication between CHA and the parents of its cadets was also addressed. A new culture of trust and support was instilled at the Academy. Simply put, God was at work to reinvigorate and reinvent an institution on the brink of closing its doors.

More important than any of the structural or cultural changes made at Chamberlain-Hunt Academy was the renewed commitment to return the institution to its Christian roots. God was returned to his rightful position. Cadet involvement in the local church was required. Where once his Word had gone mostly unnoticed at CHA, it now became the key component in the education of the cadets. Two new Bible teachers were added to the staff, and the spiritual health of the institution improved.

But for God's grace

After nearly two years on the job, I finally stepped down as President of Chamberlain-Hunt Academy. God had been good, and the differences in the institution were remarkable. The community stood up and took notice. For this service I was awarded the annual Ageless Hero Award by Blue Cross-Blue Shield of Mississippi for the accomplishments made at the Academy while I served as President. In recognition of this accomplishment, the Mississippi State Senate passed Senate Resolution Number 11 that said, in part, 'Through his vision and leadership, the future is again bright for Chamberlain-Hunt Academy.'

The words of the Board of Trustees for Chamberlain-Hunt are the ones that I cherish most, and I know that but for God's grace they would never have been written. Following the election of my successor, the Board issued this statement:

> The Board would like to express its deepest gratitude to Mr Tom Bowen for his courage and willingness to step in and assume the Presidency when French Camp Academy became the new owners of the school. History will treat Mr Bowen very kindly for his outstanding leadership, and we look forward to his continued service as a Board member.

I have continued on as a Board member for Chamberlain-Hunt Academy, and have since been asked to serve on the Board at French Camp Academy. And I am thankful to report that the improvements at Chamberlain-Hunt have continued since my resignation, further proof that I was but a means used by God in his service. Boarding student enrolment has continued to climb, and now stands at nearly

140 cadets from fifteen states. In fact, current facilities are bursting at the seams, and Chamberlain-Hunt Academy is in need of additional renovations on an existing dormitory to continue to expand. The school has received some national attention, and in 2003 the cadets were honoured by being chosen to serve as a colour guard for the President of the United States.

It is a truly remarkable story of how God used one retired man. I never sought greatness, either political or financial. I simply tried to give an honest accounting of the gifts and opportunities God entrusted to me. When I left the corporate world, I assumed that retirement would revolve around my family, my church, and the hobbies I enjoyed. I could never have imagined that, at the age of sixty-eight, God would call me into the most challenging and satisfying role of my life. Who would have guessed that my three decades at the gas company would be preparation for the presidency of a military academy? Who would have known that I would be able to give something back to a community that meant so much to my family? Who could have scripted this happy epilogue to my career? It could only have been the work of a sovereign God.

6

MATTHEW AND MURIEL MCKINNON

Matthew recalls his childhood

I was born in 1938, the youngest child of Mary and Alex McKinnon, who lived in a room and kitchen at McLellan Street in Glasgow. There were six children in our home, two girls and four boys, and like most tenements of its time it had gas lanterns for lighting, a communal toilet on the 'stair head' and a washhouse in the backcourt. The houses in McLellan Street also had the unenviable reputation of forming the longest row of unbroken tenements in Europe. My parents were first generation Christians who attended the Bethel Mission Hall at Paisley Road West. The difference Jesus brought to their lives had been so dramatic and life changing that they were determined to bring their children up to know Jesus as their personal Saviour and friend. Some of my earliest recollections were of Dad reading the Bible to us and of times spent singing Christian songs together.

Around 1941, the family was rehoused in a new council property in Glasgow's Shawlands area. A house with three bedrooms, a living room, kitchen and bathroom was luxury beyond measure, even although there was little in the way of furnishings, and varnished floor boards were gradually replaced with linoleum squares. This house became home for the family. Within weeks of arriving there all the children were enrolled in Sunday School at Greenview Hall, a Brethren Assembly in Pollokshaws, just a ten-minute walk from home. This was to be a crucial decision, as it became the spiritual home for both parents and children for many years to come. Muriel and I are still members there.

At four and a half years of age I was registered at Langside Primary School in Tantallon Road where I remained for all of my primary school education. A few short months after I started school, the McKinnon children went as usual to the children's meeting on a Friday night. The then Sunday School superintendent, Jim McLean, was giving a series of talks on *Pilgrim's Progress*, and the talks were 'illustrated by lantern slides'. When the story reached the point where Pilgrim came to the cross, and the burden of his sin fell from his back, the children were encouraged to allow Jesus to forgive their sins. On returning home my oldest brother, Alex spoke to our father about this. Before the night was over my three brothers and myself knelt at the fireplace and invited Jesus into our lives. All of us continue to serve Christ to this day.

Not long after this I was in Belvedere hospital with diphtheria, and had to spend most of that year in hospital as the diphtheria gave way to scarlet fever and then a mastoid operation. Even as a child I sensed God was with me, and with many Christians praying I eventually made a full recovery with no impairment to my hearing, which was most unusual at that time for children who underwent such an operation. I took my secondary education at Shawlands Academy. There was little encouragement at home, however, for higher education as my parents never dreamed of one of their children attending university. In those days going out to find a job was the norm! It is not surprising then that when I reached school-leaving age I left school to commence an engineering apprenticeship with Watson Laidlaw & Co. Ltd, in the south side of Glasgow.

Muriel thinks back

My background was very different. I was born in Ayr in 1937, the second daughter to my parents, Muriel and Samuel Bain. Mum suffered severe postnatal depression after my birth and was hospitalized for some time. As a result, during the first year of my life, my father's brother Charlie, and his wife Jean, who lived in Glasgow, cared for me. Dad continued to work in the Ardeer Munitions factory in Stevenston. On Mum's recovery the family came together again and moved into a new home in Saltcoats. These happy days, however, were not to last, for soon another more severe tragedy came our way. On Saturday 23 April 1939, when I was just a year and a half old, Uncle Charlie and Aunt Jean and their own two boys came through to Saltcoats for the day to visit and to see the new house. As Mum and Aunt Jean cleared up after tea, my dad and uncle went for a short run in Charlie's motor car. The car hit a kerb on a corner, somersaulted a number of times, and by the following morning the two young men lay dead in Kilmarnock Infirmary.

The first I remember was staying with Mum and my sister Rosalind at my Aunt Meg and Uncle Peter's house in the south side of Glasgow. They kindly offered us accommodation. This arrangement lasted for many years, but when my sister and I grew older we moved to other accommodation in the Battlefield area of Glasgow. I was educated at Battlefield Primary and Junior Secondary School and excelled in commercial subjects, being particularly proficient in shorthand and typing. A secretarial career throughout life resulted. My family at that time had little or no church or Christian connections, but many other activities occupied our lives. Mum, at great expense and personal sacrifice, was fully committed to training her daughters to dance. From my earliest days I recall being taken to dancing classes, mostly ballet and tap. I soon graduated to dancing with a troupe of dancers, and often did solo parts. This involved hours of practice for concerts and shows both in theatre and in exhibitions at factories and hospitals. 'Would you like to swing on a star', 'Don't fence me in' and 'Deep in the heart of Texas' were just some of the popular songs of the day to which we danced.

Throughout my childhood my best friend was Irene Gibbon, whose mum and dad had a sweet shop just below my bedroom window. Often when Mum thought I was in bed, I was in fact collecting sweets thrown up to the window. Irene, however, was instrumental in bringing to me a gift infinitely more valuable than sweets! She invited me to the Christian Youth Centre on Friday nights and to Bible Class on Sundays at Elim Hall in Glasgow. There I regularly heard the good news about Jesus and his dying love for me. One Sunday, whilst sitting alone in Queens Park prior to Bible Class, I prayed and asked Jesus to forgive my sins and to come and take control of my life. From then on life was never the same, and in her later life Mum too was to trust Jesus as her Saviour!

Matthew recalls how they met

I met Muriel at a Christian Youth Centre Camp at Largo in July 1955, and soon romance was in the air. In September 1958, we were married in Greenview Hall in Glasgow. Our first home was a room and kitchen in Pollokshaws in Glasgow, which we bought for the sum of £225.00! Over the next few years the Lord blessed us with three children: Allan, Cameron and Jennifer. That led to a few changes of address to cope with the growing family, but always in the same southside locality. Early in our married life we committed ourselves to the service of God in our local church, and so the next thirty years were spent in service, much of it working together. This involved singing in the choir, leading a hospital visitation group, being Sunday school teacher / superintendent, Bible class leader, doing youth work, youth camps, preaching, and serving as an elder which, in a brethren context, involved the full range of church pastoral responsibilities.

During the children's early years, Muriel worked as housewife and mother whilst I pursued my engineering career. This took me from the workshop floor to drawing office, and from one company to another. In 1964 I moved to A & W Smith & Co. Ltd on the south side of Glasgow, which was an engineering subsidiary of Tate & Lyle specializing in heavy equipment for the sugar industry. This was to be my place of business for the next twenty years, during which time I moved from drawing office to the management team, acting for many years as the company's Chief Estimator. In the early 1970s, this responsibility took the whole family to Mexico City for a year as the company was building a new sugar factory in the province of San Luis Potosi, and much of the equipment was being manufactured and purchased in Mexico. Later on in the 1970s, I spent two periods in Recife, Brazil doing similar work. These visits allowed an exposure to the missionary community, and as I look back I can see how the Lord was leading me into missions work.

Our move to missions took another step forward in 1980-81, when my work commitments took Muriel, Jennifer and me to Bangkok for a year. There at the Evangelical Church in Soi 10 we met the local leaders of various missions including Tearfund, OMF and Campus Crusade for Christ. During the year visits were made to the many refugee camps along the Cambodian and Burmese borders, and to a number of OMF mission stations. Some of the scenes we witnessed there were heart rending and were indelibly printed on our minds. At that time I felt sure God was directing me to a new sphere of work. On our return to Scotland I joined the Tearfund volunteer team, which involved me speaking about the work in churches across the denominations and organizing fundraising events, such as a sail on the Clyde with the paddle steamer Waverley.

Muriel shares difficulties and challenges
In the mid eighties, heavy engineering companies around the country were closing down rapidly, and Matthew was made redundant. That was a devastating experience, but God's hand was in it, as time would reveal. Matthew says that sometimes God uses drastic means to move us forward! Again the call to missions was felt, but Jennifer was still

young, and when Christian friends invited him to join their printing company in Kilsyth, Matthew took the job. This firm too, however, was soon to feel the economic pressures of the day, and within a year he was again looking for work. This time he started his own Driving School, which sponsored Tearfund, and found it to be a great form of evangelism as it provided many opportunities for speaking to students about Christ.

This drew us ever closer to the work of Tearfund and, in Keswick at the Missionary Convention meeting in 1987, we pledged ourselves (both forty-nine years of age) to go wherever God would lead. Jennifer by this time was twenty-one years old and well able to look after herself. After some cross-cultural training, we began work with Tearfund in Kenya by the following June. I was responsible for looking after Tearfund's guesthouse, which catered for workers going in and out of their stations in various parts of east and central Africa. Matthew managed the office, which was attached to the guesthouse. This entailed speaking with many African leaders regarding what help Tearfund might be able to offer, and also visiting workers, and projects of all kinds throughout the region. Many of these visits were done as a couple, and some Matthew did himself. During the next five years visits were made on numerous occasions to the slums of Nairobi, and also to projects throughout Kenya, Tanzania, Uganda, Ethiopia, Sudan, Central African Republic, Zaire (now DRC) and Rwanda. What sights, sounds and smells of Africa, what heights of joy, what depths of sorrow we witnessed. But most of all what transformations the good news about Jesus in word and deed brought to people in every situation.

During this time Matthew was also invited to serve as an elder in Nairobi Baptist Church, and to join the preaching team. I worked with the women's groups there and taught Sunday School, where I had up to ninety children IN MY CLASS! These were years of great learning for both of us. Matthew says that we went there to give of ourselves, but through our African brothers and sisters God taught us and gave us so much more in return. Unbeknown to us when we joined Tearfund, there had been for some time an ongoing debate between the Overseas Department and the Directorship regarding the advisability of having a Tearfund Overseas office in Kenya. This rumbled on and eventually came to a head at the end of 1992, when a decision was made to close the Nairobi office. Matthew felt strongly that it was the wrong decision and therefore, in June 1993, we returned to Glasgow.

Matthew tells what happened next
By then many of our contemporaries were thinking towards retirement but this was not something that either of us had on our immediate agenda. Before leaving Nairobi we compiled a list of things that we might do on our return, one of these was to speak to Mission Aviation Fellowship and to ask why they seldom spoke about their work in Scotland. On the very day that we arrived in Glasgow, the husband of my niece (who was unaware of our list) advised us that MAF were looking for someone to represent them in Scotland. Within a few short weeks I was appointed as that person. This seemed to us a sure sign that the Lord had answered our prayers and directed us into this new ministry rather than easing us in the direction of retirement!

Mission Aviation Fellowship had become well-known to us in Nairobi and also in our travels throughout East Africa. So many people relied on their support for the mission work they were involved in. Muriel had frequently visited Wilson

Airport in Nairobi from where they operated their small aircraft. These transported Tearfund workers and other mission/aid workers to the remotest parts of Africa, along with equipment, medical and food supplies. We had also used MAF to visit personnel and projects in Tanzania, Uganda and Zaire. Our overall impression of this organization was one of friendliness, helpfulness, professional efficiency, and a complete dedication to God's service.

MAF's UK office was in Folkestone in Kent, a long way from Scotland, so the work in Scotland was not so well-known. Some described MAF as the church's best kept secret. It was therefore the MAF leadership team's decision in the early 1990s to develop the work in Scotland that found me now faced with the task of leading the effort to make that decision a reality, by the help of God. Initially I worked from home, but soon premises were found in Glasgow. Prayer was to be the key to the development of MAF in Scotland. Many times the office door was shut and time was spent on my knees asking God to give wisdom and direction for the work in Scotland.

Within six months of arriving at MAF, a five-year strategy had been put in place for the advancement of the work. It seemed obvious that if Scotland had to hear about MAF in a short time, then we needed a large team of volunteers to help, and so began the task of finding, recruiting, equipping and training volunteers. Over the next ten years this team grew from a handful to a team of around one hundred people. Many of these men and women gave themselves freely and wholeheartedly to the work, and made an incredible impact for God, for missions and for MAF throughout Scotland. During this same period, the number of supporters in Scotland grew by more than fourfold, new workers were recruited for overseas service, people like the

Fothergills from Gairloch, the Milligans from Mauchline, the Boyds from Inverness, and the Wunderlis from Edinburgh. Income from Scotland also grew dramatically over the same period, and there is no doubt that the volunteer team made a significant contribution to all of that.

Muriel describes the growing work in Glasgow

When Matthew started working with MAF I was immediately called upon to help as his secretary. So whilst he benefited from my shorthand and typing and culinary skills (!) I benefited from his knowledge and zeal for computers, and have now in my sixties become proficient in their day-to-day use. Some people say that husband and wife should never work together, but we greatly enjoyed the blessing and opportunity to serve the Lord together full-time for more than fifteen years. The work was hard at times because Matthew was out a lot at nights and weekends speaking about MAF, after having spent almost every day in the office, and I accompanied him as the bookstall attendant. He also travelled on a monthly basis from Glasgow to Folkestone for meetings with the rest of the MAF UK management team under the leadership of Keith Jones, as together they worked through the implications of developing the work in Scotland. In Glasgow the staff team grew, and soon I was enjoying job sharing with Hazel Bell from Lenzie. She and I worked well together. Later we had a Trust Fundraiser, a Church Liaison Officer, and a Youth Worker. Matthew, however, felt the work took a major step forward when the MAF UK Board agreed to the setting up of a Scottish Board. This was after Alan Devereux had submitted a report to the main Board with regard to the growing work in Scotland. David Cormack from Birnam became the Board Chairman, and a number of other leaders from the Christian community readily agreed to give of their expertise. David's courses on 'Christians in Management' were of great benefit to the staff, and to the volunteers, as he often shared in their training sessions.

Matthew has been back in Africa on two occasions with MAF, once with a group of volunteers and once with Jim Tarves, the new Trust Fundraiser. These kinds of trips are so necessary to help people understand the value and significance of what MAF is about, especially if they are going to be involved in conveying the message of MAF to others. However, one day Matthew came home from the office and announced that he was taking three ladies from the Church of Scotland Guild to Papua New Guinea. 'Not without me', I announced. Not that I thought the ladies of the Guild were incapable of looking after him, but like the Guild ladies themselves I was desperate to see this project in PNG with which we had all been so busily involved. The Guild had agreed to support the work in PNG as one of their projects. So in September 2001, we set off on this very special trip, most of the group paying their own way, to see what God was doing through MAF in PNG with the help of the Guild. We stopped off at MAF's Headquarters in Melbourne, Australia on the way there, and then moved on to PNG itself. Michael Duncalfe, one of our UK pilots, and his wife Nicky, had arranged a visitation programme for us. The Guild ladies were certainly fun to be with. And in case you didn't know it – a 'WSO' stands for a 'Wee Shopping Opportunity' and they had plenty of these throughout the trip.

Fiona Lange, the Guild Information Officer, with Matthew and me, went on a five-day trip to the Western jungle. This is amongst the remotest places on earth, and it was fascinating to fly for hours over the jungle canopy, sometimes in the mist and rain, in a small five-seater aircraft, to visit missionaries working in hospitals and clinics scattered throughout the jungle. Rumginea Hospital, and its dedicated staff of doctors and nurses, working hand in hand with the MAF pilot and his wife, will live on in our memories for the rest of our lives. Not to mention the trip over the mountains into Telefomin to visit Hui Thai Tan, another MAF pilot and medical doctor who trained in Glasgow.

The most exciting part of the trip, however, was when we dropped into an isolated airstrip at Tsendiap. After having been warmly welcomed by the local people throwing flower petals at us, and given a coconut to drink, we were then shown round the mission station and Bible school. Some speeches followed under a canopy bedecked by flowers. But in the middle of Matthew's speech there was, all of a sudden, a great commotion. Half a dozen or so men emerged from the bush with large pangas and came rushing towards us in a threatening manner, shouting and screaming 'no machine, no machine'. There was a deathly silence as we, along with the local Christians, stood and stared. No one quite knew what to expect when the men blocked the aircraft in by using the cones that marked out the airstrip. After half an hour or so, however, the situation calmed and we were advised to leave as soon as possible! It let us see the volatile situations in which MAF pilots and personnel are sometimes caught up. Throughout the trip we saw countless men, women and children who had been helped by MAF and the Guild, and heard of a number of lives that had been saved. As we returned to Scotland we praised the Lord for the opportunity to see what God was able to do when Christians work together, showing the love of Christ in word and deed. Our experience in working with the Guild was one of the highlights of our service with MAF, and also it played such an important role in making MAF's work known in every town and village in Scotland.

Matthew and Muriel McKinnon

Matthew finishes their story

During the last two years of our service with MAF we were asked if we could raise money for a new aircraft for South Africa. The aircraft required was a Cessna Caravan and the amount of money to be raised in Scotland was in the region of £385,000. As we considered this, the Lord showed us from our morning readings in Nehemiah that if everyone did a little, the task could be completed. There were a number of people who seriously doubted our ability to achieve this, but God, as always, was faithful. From towns and villages throughout Scotland, from the north and the south, from the east to the western islands, people responded. By August 2002 the aircraft had been purchased, and landed in Scotland en route to Africa from America. Irene Howat from Tarbert, who had been writing the *'Scottish Special'* supplement for us over several years, supplied the name for the new aircraft. It was to be called the *Caledonian Connection*. But perhaps it was the children of the Free Church of Scotland who set the tone when they took the project to heart and raised an amazing £10,000 towards the cost. There were many inspiring efforts throughout the country to raise the money for this aircraft. Following our retirement from MAF in 2003, Muriel and I determined to visit the programme in South Africa and this visit took place in the spring of 2004. It was good to hear all the reports of how God was blessing the work being done by the help of this aircraft.

As we look back over our lives, we are grateful to God for his faithfulness through good days and difficult days, and by his grace we will continue to press on. At Keswick-in-Buckie in 2004 the Rev. Michael Baughen reminded us during the Bible Readings that no matter what age we are, we must continue to run the race. May this short story of our experience with God throughout our lives, encourage you also to keep on running. Hebrews 12:1-2 '... and let us run with perseverance the race marked out for us. Let us fix our eyes on Jesus, the author and perfecter of our faith, who for the joy set before him endured the cross, scorning its shame, and sat down at the right hand of the throne of God.'

7.

ED FORRESTER

I was born in June 1937. My father was killed in an automobile accident while I was still an infant and I was raised by my widowed mother. She had attended church when she was young and she urged us to do the same. We lived right across the street from a Lutheran church and we went there for many of the years that I was growing up in Hickory, North Carolina. I had a typical small town childhood with many wonderful companions and good experiences. The church did a lot for children, and I remember having a warm relationship with the church folks, though I really had no concept of sin or knowledge of the need to be born again.

The pressures in our home meant we all had to pull our weight, and my part was to work at whatever jobs I could find to try to bring in a few dollars. My thoughts about the Lord were very positive. I saw church people as being solid members of the community. They were substantial people who lived good lives, provided for their families and taught them well. So far as I could see those who didn't attend church weren't in the same class at all. Early on I developed a strong concept of the value of being involved in the church. But as I continued to work as much as I could, as well as study at school, I became more interested in having a good time. At the end of my sixth year of elementary school we moved to Gainesville in Georgia, because of my mother's work and the fact that her sister lived there. As a result, in my adolescence church became something of a past activity and I found my enjoyment in other things instead.

I began working in a department store, and I enjoyed the contact that gave me with the public. One of the managers, a lay Baptist minister, took an interest in me and invited me to go with him to various meetings. As a youngster I enjoyed going almost anywhere, it didn't much matter where it was. So I travelled with him and his family to meetings, and for the first time I heard what it meant to be lost, about making a decision for Christ and being saved. But at that time I was more interested in partying, which included drinking, and other things that were frankly negative.

Big changes
At the end of my junior year in high school my mother and I moved to Atlanta, Georgia. It was a really big change moving from a small town to a big city, and I found myself

getting involved in more and more negative things, the kind of things we don't like our young people to be involved in. Despite that, if I'd been asked, I would have said that I was a Christian because I'd joined the Baptist church. But I was not. When I graduated from high school in 1955, I took a full-time job in one of the large department stores in Atlanta and went to college at night. I thought I would enjoy being in sales, and my only clear ambition was to be in a full-time travelling sales position, with a company car and an expense account. I knew one or two who did that and enjoyed it. A year of so after that I met Robbie, who was to become my wife. About the same time I met her, I had the opportunity of a full-time sales job with Lever Brothers soap company. It was just what I was looking for. Perhaps it was because Robbie and I were dating at the time, but I quickly grew weary of travelling and being away from home so much. We married in December 1957, and after a little while I moved to a job in real estate that didn't involve travelling.

Soon we found ourselves setting up home in Atlanta, me in real estate and Robbie working in a bank. A former high school chum of my wife's, who was a believer, invited us to go with her to a church not far from where we lived. There she introduced us to an older couple who were to have a big impact on us. The husband was the choir director and his wife taught in Sunday School. Their names were Herm and Pat Logan. They were truly committed to the Lord Jesus, living for him and basing their lives and decisions on him. The Lord used them to show us that was the right way to live. They began to share with us the truth of the scriptures and the need to have a personal relationship with the Lord. Eventually, in a Bible teaching session, my wife and I both committed ourselves to the Lord at the same time. Till then Robbie, like me, had been just a nominal Christian.

We were very blessed in that church because God's Word was clearly and beautifully taught there, and young Christians were counselled and mentored. Although we were struggling to make ends meet, at the same time we were happy and growing in the Lord. It was during this time that Pat Logan challenged me to teach a young boys' class in church. I accepted the position and found myself really enjoying it, especially the preparation involved. And I also discovered what a wonderful thing it is to share God's Word and see people responding to it. Robbie and I became deeply involved with high school young folk in church: teaching, taking retreats, study sessions, seeing the Lord do great things in their lives. As they grew up and married, we continued to work with them through a young couples' class that the Lord blessed tremendously.

New commitments

In 1962, the choir director, who worked for the Prudential Insurance Company, approached me about the possibility of joining the company and working under his management. I did that, and after a few struggling years began to reap some of the benefits of that business. Four years later our only child, Scott was born. It was a busy life, with Scott, church and career. After a while another area of involvement presented itself when I was asked to join the board of a Christian and Missionary Alliance School. Dekalb Christian Academy was committed to Christian education, and as we also saw that as a priority we enrolled Scott in that school. Our involvement there took up a great deal of our time, as did our work within the church. By then we were members of the Christian and Missionary Alliance church to which the school was attached, and before long I was asked to teach a group there. Although there were challenges going on in our lives that sometimes tempted us not to walk as carefully as we should have done, overall those years were positive times of growth.

After sixteen years as a sales agent with the Prudential, an opportunity arose to become manager of an Atlanta office. That began the latter half of my career with the company. I found myself working with some men whom I had known for years, many of them were believers deeply committed to Christ. There were negatives and challenges along the way, but there was also the clear hand of God's blessing. Through all of that time our lives were centred round our relationship with Christ, our teaching work in the church and our involvement in the Christian Academy. That doesn't mean that there were no problems. There were many times in our walk with the Lord when we were unfaithful or discouraged, or grew cold in our relationship with him. We went through phases when we became somewhat disenchanted. Yet looking back we see how faithful the Lord was even when we were unfaithful. Often the Lord used the fact that I had to teach a class to bring me closer to himself, as I was forced to study his Word by way of preparation. Several times in my life that need has brought me through times of staleness back into a more vibrant relationship with my Saviour. The number one thing God has used in my life has been teaching, not because I'm a great teacher, but when you are teaching you are committed to learning yourself.

Early retirement
When I was fifty-seven years old, the Lord brought the opportunity to retire. The company was down-sizing and those, like me, who had been around a long time were offered a package of benefits that allowed us to retire. I had worked for the company for thirty-two years and felt it was time to

move on. It was then that I began to develop serious heart problems. Having jogged for years, I found myself out of breath going downhill! Also, when golfing I seemed to be suffering from indigestion that was relieved by a rest and a soft drink. I thought I was just stressed by my recent retirement. Then, in July 1994, when one of these incidences hit me on the golf course and I nearly lost consciousness, I realized something more serious than stress was the problem. When I went to the doctor he found I had blockages in one or more blood vessels round my heart. After various ups and downs I found myself having quadruple bypass surgery just short of a year later. God has been very good to me as I've had no further problems since then.

Looking back, I think that 1994–5 was a time of treading water, not doing anything much and just moving along and becoming used to the whole business of retirement. It was a time of reflection, and one of the conclusions Robbie and I came to was that we should consider looking for a second home down on the Georgia coast. As a result we built a little patio home in Savannah, in an area called The Landings. Thinking we would keep our house in Atlanta and move back and forward between the two, we began to settle into a typically retired lifestyle. I was not teaching then, and because of the move we were a little bit loose in our church situation. I think we both felt just a tiny bit lost. However, we joined a church close to where we lived and began to become involved.

The word got out that I taught Scripture, and first one request then another came for me to teach. My initial thought was that I was retired and it was time for someone else to do what I had done. But having prayed about it, I sensed that wasn't right and accepted teaching short studies here and there. About that time Rev. John Stott, from London, came to Savannah to speak, and we went to hear him. At the meeting we met a lovely lady called Betty Myers who attended the church in which the meeting was held, and who lived near us. She and her husband, Alan became friends, and their friendship was a special blessing as we were still quite new to the area. When we knew each other a little better, Betty asked if I would be willing to teach a Bible study in her home if she took the responsibility of hosting it and letting people know it was on. Alan and Betty had benefited from a short-term home Bible study they had attended and could see the value of such a venture.

Prison ministry

Robbie and I prayed about it and agreed it would be a good idea. That Bible study went on weekly for four years, and we saw God's power and grace in the lives of those who attended it. Some really got into the Word and discovered for themselves its changing and transforming power. During that same time I heard about a ministry in the Chatham County Jail through Max Baldwin, one of the men in our Bible Study, who was involved in it. He was invited by our church to make a presentation to any who were interested. I went to it and was very taken with what I heard. I remember thinking what a good and beneficial ministry it was, though I had no thought of becoming involved. Max saw my interest and said he'd like to introduce me to Johnny Hands, the prison chaplain. Soon afterwards Max brought Johnny to our Bible study and we were glad to have him there with us. As it never occurred to me that Max thought I might become part of the prison ministry, it came as a surprise when two or three weeks later Mr Hands phoned and asked me to meet with him to consider the possibility of becoming a volunteer in their chaplains' programme. We met to discuss it and Robbie and I prayed about it. God led us to see that this was what he meant me to do, and I started going to the jail one day a week to teach Scripture. That was how it started.

The Good News Jail and Prison Ministry, which is based in Richmond, Virginia, staffs prisons with chaplains. If a jail invites Good News they will staff that facility at no cost to the jail, which is then free to use the money they might have spent on chaplains' services on other things. Of course, there is another advantage to this arrangement, and that is that the chaplains maintain their independence. Chatham County Jail has about 1,400 inmates housed in five wings. Each wing has four dormitories running from a central hub, and each of these dormitories has 50–60 inmates. The Sheriff asked Good News Jail and Prison Ministry to provide chaplains, and designated Wing 3, Dorm D as chaplains' dorms where those undertaking the Ministry's programme would be housed. Prisoners have to agree to a very structured programme of study. Some of that is personal study using student sheets, Bible studies, book reports and questionnaires. Additional to that they have to attend teaching sessions each day, Monday through Friday.

When I went on board, two chaplains were trying to teach the whole programme, but it was far too much for them. Apart from the teaching they were required to do, they had pastoral responsibility for the entire jail, officers and inmates. My coming in to help with the teaching freed them up to devote a little of their time and attention to other things. I was asked to teach one day a week, and I began that in 1999. I very quickly found that this was something that was not only interesting and continued to use the teaching skills that the Lord seems to have given me, but it was also interesting from the point of view that I'd never taught in such a setting, and the interaction I was able to have with the inmates was different to any I had had before. Because I had the time, I not only taught but was able to engage with some of the men on a one-to-one basis.

A learning experience

In a county jail there is every kind of inmate, from those who have committed minor offences to those awaiting trial for murder. I learned many things, and one of them is that the Lord showed me that there is basically no difference between the men whom I met as prison inmates and other citizens. Many of these men have been in churches and many believe they are Christians. Some of them have joined churches and think that means they are saved. There are those among them who are born again, but who have little or no in-depth knowledge of God's Word. They don't usually come from churches where the scriptures are taught verse by verse, but often from congregations where more stress is put on emotional responses. I began to see that the dynamics are the same inside and outside of jail.

It is a privilege to be part of a ministry that allows the free teaching of the Word of God. But what we do, we have to do quickly, as the average inmate is only on our programme for no more than six months, maybe less. A few are there longer, but that is unusual. The chaplains have constructed their programme to cover the essential areas of the Christian faith within a period of four to six months. The programme includes showing what the Bible says about the need to be born again, how to become a Christian, and the basics of living the Christian life. I was very happy to be involved in teaching that programme. Before long the chaplains asked me to consider giving two days a week to the work. That was easy to do as I didn't have many other commitments, and I was physically fine by then. Also I very much enjoyed the work. When I went two days each week I taught the same lesson twice, once in each of the two chaplains' dorms. Then the lady who was head of the dorm that works towards drug and alcohol rehabilitation using the Alcoholics Anonymous programme, asked if I would make a presentation during one of their graduation ceremonies. I was very happy to accept that invitation. That work is not part of the Good News Ministry. Following that she invited me to do a weekly Bible study with her group of prisoners over and above my commitment to the other chaplains' dorms. My retirement was filling up, but in a way that Robbie and I felt good about. It is much more fulfilling than playing a round of golf every day.

One problem Robbie and I had was that we had to drive too much. Our home was in rather a remote area, and everywhere we went we had to take the car. We were also very attracted to the Independent Presbyterian Church in Savannah, where the minister is Rev. Terry Johnston. And at that time we were feeling restless in our congregation. The Lord seemed to be showing us that it was time to move. He confirmed our move by providing us with buyers for our home as well as our Atlanta house, and leading us to a more suitable condominium in downtown Savannah near the Independent Presbyterian Church, and much nearer the jail. We were accepted into church membership and we have never looked back. Our minister's ability to preach the reformed faith has done us good in heart, mind and soul.

Settled

Robbie had been unsettled after our first move, but since moving closer into town she has made so many friends that she now feels at home in Savannah. After we moved the prison chaplain asked if I would consider adding a third day to my prison work, and I agreed to do that. By then I was teaching in the chaplains' dorms three days a week and the drug and alcohol rehabilitation dorm one day a week. I am also privileged to have responsibilities within the congregation. In 2003 I was voted a ruling elder and began a six-year term of service. The congregation is divided into care groups and each elder is responsible for the spiritual welfare of the people in his care group. We keep in touch with them, pray for them and try to minister to their needs and encourage their spiritual growth. Of course, the eldership also involves committees and other work. Some of my fellow elders are still working, and I realize how little time they have compared to me. I really enjoy having the time to do these things without having to juggle it with work. Recently the jail ministry expanded and now I'm there for two hours on Monday mornings, all morning Tuesdays, and two hours on Thursdays and Fridays. Wednesdays I keep free, and Robbie and I need that.

I hoped that I'd be able to use my time well in retirement, and I now find myself with a work schedule that suits me fine. I love the opportunity to be busy about something that really counts and has a purpose. Although my schedule is demanding, it is not overly so. I know myself well enough to realize that if I didn't have to prepare my teaching material I would not discipline myself to study. There have been times in my life when I drifted in my discipleship because I let the discipline of study go. I don't think that even in retirement we need excessive amounts of time in idleness, or golf! No amount of success on the golf course could compare with seeing men's lives drastically changed as they come to know the Lord. I hope and pray that when they enter society again, they will be able to bear a strong, good and clear testimony to the Lord. Having said that, it would be unrealistic to give the impression that all who go through the programme come to a saving faith. Sadly, they do not. But we rejoice over those who do, and what could be more gratifying than that for a retiree like me.

8.

PETER MORRISON

What would you do if you had the opportunity of living your life all over again? Although I did not understand at the time, there are not many changes I would make, apart from undoing my mistakes, which would be a big task.

Born in Fort William, Inverness-shire, a few months before the outbreak of the Second World War, I spent the first six years of my life there before my father was transferred to a post in Dingwall in Ross-shire. One of my earliest memories was seeing my grandmother take in the hay on the croft in Skye, in what seemed to me to be huge bundles. It was only much later that I came to realise what backbreaking work was involved in mere survival in Scotland's West Highland crofting communities ... and women did much of it. The first year of my school life was in Fort William. One year later, on enrolling me at school in Dingwall, my mother was told by the stern infant mistress that she was ruining her son's life by letting him continue to write with his left hand. So, at the tender age of six, I was forced to start learning to write with my right hand. Now, many years later, that is about the only thing I do with my right hand apart from shaking hands. Did the boy suffer psychological damage that has impaired his whole development? I'll never know, but I am happy that the days of such ignorance from teachers are a distant memory.

School was not bad, but few cherished memories of it remain. There were the good teachers, but also the few who were blind to the needs of children, particularly those who seemed to be having difficulties with some aspect of learning. Like so many of my fellows, I left school without distinction, but not entirely. After all, I was first equal in Latin in 6th Year. The only problem was that there were only two in the class! Shortly before leaving, I told the Rector of Dingwall Academy that I had been accepted for university. His response was, 'No doubt, Morrison, you will have your setbacks'. His comment was not exactly geared either to praise or encourage me, but in a strange way I am grateful to him for it. By his lack of enthusiasm he taught me how important it is to encourage people. When I went into teaching that most important lesson remained with me.

Scripture Union

One of the great features of growing up in Easter Ross in the 1950s was the influence of Scripture Union. Most schools had branches, and many young folk were given some of their first insights into the Christian faith at the SU meeting, and many came to a living faith in Jesus Christ at SU camps. Dingwall Academy was no exception and, under the faithful leadership of the late Neil MacLeod and others, generations of young folk were influenced for Christ. Along with this there was church life. We were blessed with the gracious ministry of Duncan Leitch, who had a worldwide view of Christ's Kingdom, which enriched his local ministry. Through a combination of these elements, and a home where Christianity was for real, I was drawn to have faith in Christ. Perhaps it would be better to say that he laid his hand on me.

On leaving school I went to Edinburgh University, where I distinguished myself no more than at school. The learning curve was very steep, and I suppose that I should be glad that I left with no distinctions, but with an appalling sense of ignorance. I hope this sense of ignorance has stood me in good stead and has saved me, to some small extent, from being over-dogmatic. Only others can judge that. After completing teacher training in Moray House, Edinburgh, in the summer of 1963, I started teaching in Bellahouston Academy in Glasgow. These early memories were seared into my mind. If we were told anything in Moray House about how to handle children, I certainly did not remember it. Bellahouston Academy had formerly been a senior secondary school that only took pupils from the top half or so of the ability range, but not long before I joined the staff it was made comprehensive. The fact that new pupils came in spanning the whole range of ability seemed not to have dawned on the management, and that left the new recruit not only without advice, but without a curriculum for those recently absorbed pupils. With no room of my own life was very often a nightmare. But I kept going, encouraged by the fact that the Depute Head, also Principal Teacher of Geography, asked me to take his Higher class until he had finished the timetable. Keeping one lesson ahead of the pupils, this class helped me to feel that work was not all a struggle. It took me only a little time to realize that if the Depute Head had not finished the timetable the school simply could not function!

Enter Marion

Gradually life in school improved and I began to see beyond the jungle – which probably existed in my mind only – to the higher ground of gaining insight into the needs of the pupils, of seeing the importance of relationships and looking upon even what I felt was a bad pupil as a real person. On the subject of relationships, those days were brightened by a new one, with Marion, whose roots were so similar to my own, which culminated in our marriage in July 1968. Our honeymoon in Harris, at Seilebost, near the Isle of Taransay, was not everyone's dream ... thankfully. So quiet were the glorious beaches that we resented the presence of even a speck on the horizon. And the simple cottage, recently inherited by Marion's father from her grand-uncles, to this day reminds us that happiness has nothing to do with the things we possess. We set up home in East Kilbride and saw our son born in 1970 and daughter in 1972.

Changes of workplace within the education system brought me into contact with fairly challenging situations where survival, rather than education, was the priority for the pupils. The challenge still remains, and the most exciting thing that could happen to our education system would be to see pupils motivated to be eager for learning. I am sure that in the majority of cases it is lack of motivation, rather than lack of ability, that is the hindrance to achievement.

In 1984 I was appointed Head Teacher of Woodside Secondary School, which served the west of the centre of Glasgow. Previously I had been Depute Head there for some years. There followed an exciting decade of dealing with a multitude of persons, issues and developments. Half the school pupils were of Asian origin, children of first or second generation immigrants. The mutual enrichment of such a school environment was precious and opened up a whole range of contacts, the vast majority of which were delightful.

No regrets

Life suddenly changed in 1994 when the process of readjustment of school provision in the city involved a language-teaching unit closing down and being absorbed into our school building. Teachers over fifty-five years of age, in both the closing and receiving establishments, were given the special offer of up to ten years enhancement of pension rights if they applied for early retirement. That was an offer I could not refuse. I either had to go then or work for another nine years. With considerable reluctance I decided to retire, deciding it was better to do that than to leave nine years later, with more folk than ever feeling that it was time for 'him' to go. There followed for Marion and me one of the most remarkable periods of our lives together. If the way had not opened up in a new and fascinating direction I might have regretted my decision to retire then. But a way did open before us, and soon!

Weeks after retiring there appeared in the Free Church of Scotland's magazine, *The Monthly Record*, an advertisement for the part-time post of Overseas Missions Secretary. I was immediately challenged and thought long about the matter, and prayed about it too. As so often happens when we look for guidance in life, there was no great revelation, rather the sense that I ought to do something about it, that I had to push the door open to discover if it was the right way forward. I did that by applying for the post knowing that it was up to the selection committee, rather than to me, to judge my suitability as a candidate. To a degree it concerned me that I might be denying the job to somebody who needed the employment more, but I soon came to realize for myself what I had so often stressed in my previous employment, that the person is for the job and not the job for the person. Many a bad appointment has been made just for the sake of giving somebody a job.

Time and again in the ensuing years I was to witness that our response to a perceived need or opportunity should be only to a small extent controlled by our feelings. If the Lord shows a need or an opportunity, who are we to say that the fact that we do not feel like pushing the door open is a reason for inaction? In this age of 'if it feels good, do it' mentality the Christian way remains clear: 'Go, in my name.' Looking for blinding lights in seeking a way forward can be a less reliable guide than the considered approaches of committed persons. It has been an immense privilege to witness time and again the ready response of ministers and church members to the requests of the Missions Board to undertake work in far from congenial circumstances.

What the job involved

A background in educational work was, I suppose, a good preparation for being Secretary to the Foreign Missions Board (it was soon to become the International Missions Board). Much of the work was concerned with personnel matters: processing job applications, supporting staff, and reporting on various activities and developments and promoting the work with the supporters. Almost every aspect of the work was rewarding, but none more so than having the privilege of passing on what was happening overseas to supporters in various congregations and missionary-minded groups. Much of the Board Secretary's work was administrative, servicing the needs of personnel working overseas and their families, often at home in Scotland. This age of electronic communication made it possible to be in touch with every corner of the world at a speed unimaginable just a few years ago. The Internet has done much to lessen the isolation of missionaries, making it possible for some to get the results of football matches as soon as the final whistle sounds, information of doubtful value in many instances! However, effective reviewing of the work could only take place by actually visiting the areas of operation.

The Free Church has its long-established areas of missionary operation in India, South Africa and Peru. Wisely, many years ago, responsibility for the work was given to the local churches with which the Church works in partnership. For example, the last missionaries in India had to leave in 1988, but the ministry has continued with Indian personnel in both church and hospital work. The latter has grown in a wonderful way with the Emmanuel Hospital Association. In the course of my work as Secretary to the Board it was my privilege to visit all three areas of current and former missionary work, and Marion was able to go with me. This involved quite strenuous schedules and was far from being a holiday. But to witness the work, and to see the conditions under which it took place, and still takes place, left us with a sense of wonder at the sustaining grace of God that enables people to go on working, sometimes in quite extraordinary situations. I discovered that from the safety of the U.K. it is very easy to misinterpret the actions and attitudes of those working in situations we don't understand. How would I behave if I had to face the challenges that meet so many Christians in developing countries? When I think of the people we met on our travels, people who gave their all in God's service, I find myself wondering what my faith costs me here in Britain.

El Nino

In Peru, when the El Nino disaster struck in 1998, savage floods devastated huge areas of the land, and concrete irrigation channels were tossed around like pieces of straw. Silt carried down from the mountains accumulated behind dams, so that there was no room to store water. In some instances communities were relocated to inhospitable desert areas. Dr Apollos Landa, of the Associacion San Lucas, and some local pastors took us around some of the affected areas. Never will we forget the pastor of one village near the northern city of Trujillo. Totally identified with his flock, he moved with them to live in a flimsy straw shelter in the desert. A short time earlier we had seen the last remnants of his village church building crumbling into a stream that had deposited millions of tons of rubble over the once-productive fields. When informed of the needs, the response from the churches in Scotland was very encouraging. So much money was donated to help the people in the Trujillo area that the pastors were able to pass some on to the church in Chiclayo for their needy.

One of the most exciting things about the work of the gospel is the ripple effect that defies time and distance. Seated in the home of a doctor in the northern Peruvian town of Trujillo, we listened in wonder as he told us his story. Many years earlier, in his home town of Cajamarca, his mother had no peace in her mind and she went and explained her problem to a local religious leader. As he had nothing to offer she went to the missionary, the late Rev. Malcolm Macrae. Mr Macrae told the woman that of himself he could do nothing for her, but that he knew who could. He pointed the woman to Christ and she became a believer and witnessed to the Lord's transforming power. One by one her family was led to the Lord. Years later, in Trujillo, long after the passing of both her and the missionary concerned, her son was not only doing medical work, but had opened a church. We had gone to Peru to have discussions with church leaders and our own missionary personnel in an effort to support them further, and on behalf of the Board to attempt some evaluation of our support. These things we at least attempted to do, but the impact of what we witnessed made us the learners in a way we never anticipated. Our support, usually expressed in financial terms, appeared a paltry offering compared to the total dedication of so many Peruvian Christians.

Next stop India

With a similar review remit we went to Madhya Pradesh State in India, where we witnessed the fruits of long and faithful missionary service in medicine and in the churches. The work still went on, but fully in Indian hands with support from churches in Scotland. There is still a long way to go before they can be financially self-sufficient, and there are huge challenges facing Christians, but the question kept coming back to us, What would I be like, if I lived in these circumstances? The biggest challenge has nothing to do with finance. It is the fact that when a Hindu or Muslim turns to Christ he or she can be as good as dead as far as the family is concerned. We felt very deeply for Dr Latta, the lovely young doctor in Lakhnadon Hospital who was disowned by her family because she became a Christian. In a land where arranged marriages are still very common it means that marriage prospects are slender. This is service at a cost that we cannot experience. Some time after our visit in 2000, Dr Latta was at a medical conference and there, totally unexpectedly, she met another young doctor who was to become her husband! Now they are a family of four, and meetings have taken place with estranged relatives. It was a privilege to tell about Dr Latta on our return from India, to witness the concern and prayer of so many folk in Scotland, and then to be able to tell of the happy developments later. Some friends in the Isle of Lewis so took her to their hearts that a warm relationship has been built up through correspondence.

In Manipur State we witnessed the growth of the Reformed Presbyterian Church of North East India. An invitation had been extended to our Board to send representatives to meet with the people. There was little Western influence and we just felt like spiritual dwarves. How can anyone from the West respond to the church leader who, when talking about evangelism, said 'Manipur is only 25 percent Christian, we have to be missionaries!'? We could only hang our heads in shame. What could we say in response? Almost free from a dependency culture, that church, in one of the poorest parts of India, fully supports its own pastors.

Emerging from Apartheid
South Africa was emerging from the Apartheid state when we visited it towards the end of 1996. What could we say of a regime that left so many disenfranchised? Apart from the compulsive need to learn from history, there was no compelling reason to dwell on the past. The Africans themselves, and we do not claim the society is perfect, provided one of life's most powerful lessons about human

dignity in adversity. They emerged from awful huts, made out of flattened oil drums, dressed immaculately. They shake hands in a way that we cannot even begin to imitate. They harmonize in singing with a natural skill that provides one of the finest sounds imaginable. How deaf were the ears of the minority! They provided for us bountifully out of their poverty, and it was a privilege to partake of their hospitality. Again, the review and reporting purpose of our visit was fulfilled in a context where we were the ones who were learning about commitment and contentedness in particular. There are tremendous challenges facing the church in South Africa, particularly the rural parts of the former Transkei, where the menfolk of communities are so often away from home to find work and there are enormous issues of sexual morality.

These examples are just a tiny section of the experiences that we had, I dare not say 'enjoyed', because for the most part we felt like worms. It was a privilege to share these experiences with a variety of audiences and to witness a caring and prayerful response at the home end. We do hope that in some measure they fulfilled their purpose in a better targeting of the Board's support, and in the stimulation of interest at the home end. It would take many chapters to tell the whole story of the years with the International Missions Board.

What else has happened? Recently a colleague on a school board asked me if I played golf. When I explained my lack of skill and participation he said, 'What else is there to life?' I knew he was half-joking, but I could not help thinking how empty life would be if it were dominated by golf. Because of my involvement in education I was asked over two years ago to help with the development of a college in Northern Bangladesh. This has provided yet another dimension to life.

It was an amazing experience to visit the country and to be greeted so hospitably, and as in so many other places, to learn of the incredibly challenging situations which ordinary people face. There have been other involvements, such as school board activities and serving on the committee of management for a housing association.

Age does not really matter

The rest of my time? There is not enough of it. When time permits I love to work with wood. So long ago in Dingwall Academy the late Neil Macleod taught us how to use a saw and cut joints. Many years later, in my retirement, he was not only the oldest member of the International Missions Board, but indisputably the one with the most detailed interest in every aspect of missionary work. Neil Macleod showed me that age does not really matter, and he is not the only example of those who show vigour and enthusiasm into their advanced years. After so many years in school I have met more elderly teenage couch potatoes than those who have many years behind them.

Blessed with grandchildren, and hosts of friends and interests, there is absolutely nothing to complain about. I just hope I will have the sense to pull out of a pursuit before others might think 'he' has passed the sell-by date. In this, of course there is the great comfort that our times are in Bigger Hands and the absolute assurance that all will be well ... and perfectly timed. To family annoyance I quote Browning's *Rabbi Ben Ezra:*

Grow old along with me!
The best is yet to be,
The last of life, which for the first was made:

Our times are in His hand
Who saith 'A whole I planned,
Youth shows but half; trust God: See all, nor be afraid.'

Better, of course, to remember the words of the prophet Ezekiel, 'I will ... do better to you than at your beginnings; and you shall know that I am the Lord' (Ezek. 36:11, AV).

9.

JOAN HALL

Each of our backgrounds is special and different. I was brought up in a home where we were loved and cared for. Our parents did what they could, despite a tight budget, to educate us and look after us. However, ours was a very religious home. There was no laughter on a Sunday, nor balls or toys of any sort allowed. We were allowed to read *Pilgrim's Progress* or the Bible, and we were allowed to write letters and to use coloured crayons! Most of our relatives wore dark clothes and had long hair. Things like using make-up or wearing slacks were never allowed. And, of course, behind all the rules was a belief system. My parents were members of a small, narrow and rigid denomination in which new and innovative things had no place, unless they were 'new' a hundred years ago.

When I was a child we moved from place to place quite a lot because of evacuation during the Second World War. We were also used to travelling quite long journeys to chapel. There were five in our family, my parents, my two younger sisters and me, and we often made up half of the congregation wherever we went, as many of the congregations in our denomination were very small indeed. Long sermons were often read from books, and my memory is that we sang very slowly. Some of our chapels had no instrumental music at all. As a child I had difficulty understanding the sermons; later I discovered that my parents had too. Having opted out of listening to sermons, I spent my time adding up hymn numbers and watching the hands of the clock moving round, or not. Meetings for young people were unheard of.

During the war, when Doodle Bugs were flying round New Malden on the outskirts of London, where we then lived, and buildings were frequently destroyed, the vicar of the local Anglican Church came to visit us. Before he left, he invited us to go to his church. My parents thanked him warmly for coming to visit us, but assured him that we would not be attending his church. However, they were struck by his sincerity, and it may be that in their heart of hearts they could see that the chapels we were attending had little to offer to us children.

The beginning of change
On one Sunday morning soon after his visit it was pouring with rain. We left for Chapel and waited for the red bus to

come to take us there. The bus stop was exactly opposite the church from which the vicar had come to visit us. No bus came, and the deluge of rain continued. We were getting drenched! 'The bus does not seem to be coming,' said Father. 'So let us go into this church. We will sit at the back, and you are to do what I do. You are not to say any of the set prayers!' Father was a tall, large person, some six foot two inches tall, and we did not argue with him. Prepared to obey his instructions, we set off through the puddles and across the road. I was scared as I had never been in an Anglican church before. I'm still not quite sure what I thought might happen to us there. What a difference! The church was full, and it was quite hard to find seats! We received a warm welcome and my parents found that they could understand the sermon. That day marked the beginning of a change in our family life.

One of the first sermons that we heard there was on, 'You are accepted in the Beloved!' (Eph. 1:6 AV). My mother was very touched by what she heard that day as she had been brought up to believe that she could not have assurance of salvation. That was considered to be presumption. Mother had committed her life to Christ as a young girl, but had never been really sure that she belonged to him, and she certainly did not feel accepted by God. That sermon changed her completely. Throughout the rest of her life Mother was assured that she belonged to the Lord, and that she was loved and accepted by him through Jesus the Beloved.

We found that there was a flourishing young people's group in the church and I attended it. On Easter Day 1945, I asked Jesus Christ into my life. The following day the young people went on a ramble. As we walked, the curate asked me when I was going to commit my life to Christ. I told him that I had done so the previous day. 'Right,' he said, 'then next Sunday you can tell us all about it!' I knew a joy that I had never known before. God's presence stayed with me, and he was a great strength to me during the O level exams that I took shortly afterwards.

Missionary interest

Another great change we experienced in our new church was in the attitude to sharing one's faith, both personally and in the area of missionary work. In the previous denomination missionaries were unheard of. We were told that, 'If God wants to bring somebody to himself, he will, and there is nothing we can do about it.' However, the church we had started to attend took a keen interest in missionary activity, in particular in the then Ruanda Mission that worked in South West Uganda, Rwanda and Burundi. My parents subscribed to the Ruanda Mission Magazine. Ruanda is now known as Rwanda. The Mission was then called Ruanda Mission, CMS (Church Mission Society). It then changed to Rwanda Mission, CMS, before becoming Mid Africa Ministry, CMS, then eventually being incorporated into CMS.

Having trained as a Primary School teacher, I had to do two years on probation before being fully qualified. One evening, before I had completed my probationary period, I was baby-sitting for a friend. The child obliged by sleeping and I read through the Mission magazine. One article hit my heart. It described the need for a primary school teacher at Kabale in South West Uganda, in a school for missionaries' children. That very night I had a strong sense that God wanted me to apply for the post. I talked with family, friends and my vicar about my feelings, and the deep conviction that I should at least write to the Mission and enquire about the post. Application forms came and were completed ... but I was frightened to put them in the post! They sat, completed, in my room for a whole month. Eventually I plucked up courage and posted them. As I did so I had a great sense of relief. Then came the waiting time.

I was called for interviews, plural! One big thing was against me. I had had a very bad health history, having had several operations and long spells ill at home, both as a child and as a teenager. My aunt said, 'We do not even need to pray for you because we know that no missionary society will accept you with the poor health you have had.' To the horror of my parents and relatives the Mission forgot to give me a medical, and I was accepted for 'short service', which at that time was for four years! It was cheaper to go by boat than to fly, and I spent twenty-one days travelling from London to Kampala.

Kabale

Getting to Africa was one thing, getting to Kabale was quite another. But after a hair-raising journey I found myself at Kabale Preparatory School, with bougainvillaea laid on the ground to form the words 'Welcome to Auntie Joan.' The school was small, and all staff members were referred to as aunties. I was made to feel so welcome by fellow missionaries, Ugandan staff and Ugandans who worked there. God has been amazingly good in the people he has brought alongside me on life's path. I am so grateful to those who were in Uganda before me who, all unknowing, set about shaping my life. Alongside them were our Ugandan colleagues and friends. I believe that our Ugandan Christian friends were concerned about the spiritual life of some of us missionaries, and so every Monday after school lessons were over there was an English Bible Study. I did not know the local language at that point.

Challenged

After four years I returned on leave to England. 'Short Service' was behind me, and during my time back home I did some missionary training then returned to Uganda to head up Kabale Girls' Primary School. It was mainly a day school, but there were about thirty-five boarders as well as the day girls. Whilst at the Primary School I began to be challenged about my life as a Christian. One Ugandan Christian said to me, 'Joan, when you get so angry we do not see Jesus in you.' An elderly uneducated lady came and sat in my sitting room and said, 'Sometimes we feel sorry for you missionaries. You seem to know Jesus in your heads, but we know him in our hearts.' Then there was Charles the tailor, with his round beaming face, who said, 'You look so miserable, Joan. Didn't Jesus die for you?'

The problem was not that I had never come to Christ and asked him to be my Saviour. It lay in the fact that I did not know what to do with my reactions, with anger and with myself. I continued with my daily Bible readings and quiet time, with church attendance and witnessing, but inwardly I was aware that there was spiritual dearth. I was spiritually dry. When I looked at the folk around me, I saw many who were like the Christians of 2 Corinthians 8:2. 'Their overflowing joy and their extreme poverty welled up in rich generosity.' My career would have taken a very different course had I not begun to learn what to do with my past, my attitudes and my reactions.

Somehow the Holy Spirit began to remind me of things that could not be joined together. He reminded me that I had been Secretary to the Christian Union when I was at college. I had not done the job very well, and so had put the Secretary's minute book in my trunk. It sat there for years and years, and I completely forgot about it. But the Spirit of

Truth had not forgotten about it. I looked in my trunk and there was the book. I found it hard to own up to the fact that I had not done my work properly, but eventually packed the book up and sent it with apologies to the college in which I had trained.

Then there was the matter of school fees that parents brought and gave to me. I put the money in my pocket and used it for purchasing eggs and cabbages and whatever else was needed. There were no accurate records, and I used school fees for my personal purchases. The Lord asked me how I thought I could mix the oil of the Holy Spirit of Truth with my lack of integrity. How could I expect to have his fruit in my life? I began to realize that I could not mix these things, and that I would have to confess them. But what would the Mission say? What about the parents? What would they say when they knew that I had been misappropriating the school's money? I was really scared, especially as I thought that the Mission might ask me to go back to the UK. Not only that, but I feared that the parents of the school's pupils could make life very difficult for me.

How gracious God is! I began to understand that Jesus could deal with my life if I was willing to stand up for the truth about myself. Not only that, but I also understood for the first time that 'the Blood of Jesus cleanses from all sin.' I found that I could trust him with the consequences of following him. Consequently, I confessed my sin and asked those concerned to forgive me. As a result I learned in a new way that the devil IS the father of lies. All the fears he had put in my heart were ungrounded. The parents put their trust in me, and after my next leave the Mission sent me to work at Bweranyangi Secondary School in Ankole, about 100 miles away. I began to learn from my own experience, as well as from an understanding of theology, that Jesus takes away sin and guilt, and replaces it with his abundant life in all its fullness.

Time to move

Did I want to move away from Kabale, where I had been so blessed and made so many friends? I definitely did not. It took me a long time to agree with God about being posted to the other school. It was some four years before I decided to 'agree with God and be at peace with him'. When I found myself headmistress of a secondary school going up to O level, one Ugandan suggested that I should go and study for a degree. However, we were seeing a time of deep blessing in the school, and I felt that if I left at that point I might never see anything like it again. I also felt that I could trust the Lord with my future even though I did not have a degree. And the future he had in store for me was eleven years in that school then a few months at Kyebambe Secondary School in Fort Portal, that was about to start taking students up to university entrance standard. Family illness then made it necessary for me to return to England.

Soon after I arrived back in the UK, my father passed away. My sister continued to be sick, and so it was that I remained in the UK and was invited to be Travelling Secretary for the Rwanda Mission, and subsequently became Home Secretary and Acting General Secretary. These posts enabled me to keep in touch with Uganda as I went back to see the work at first hand about every eighteen months. It never crossed my mind that I would ever return to Uganda to work. Some time later God gave me a really surprising career change. I was invited to introduce the subject of Mission into a theological college: Cranmer Hall, St John's College, Durham. Then came retirement in 1990.

Back to Africa

I bought a flat in Exeter with the thought of retiring there. But no sooner had I arrived to begin my retirement, than the Mission asked if I would go with a doctor to Rwanda and Tanzania to assess the situation in the theological colleges and Bible colleges, and in the hospital and health units following the holocaust there. It was moving to see the thousands of refugees in the camps. Words cannot describe it. On arrival back to U.K., I told someone that I thought that I would never be back in Africa again. How wrong can you be! One day a friend living not far from Exeter asked me if there was anything tangible to show for the fact that the East African Revival had been greatly used of God? Having the subject sown in my mind, eventually the idea of a book germinated and began to grow. However, as I do not aspire to being an author, I offered to do some research on the understanding that someone else would write the book. I went back to Uganda to research for *Pioneers in the East African Revival.*

The Lord has had much to teach me about willingness to go where he wants me to be. I went into a home, and on the dining room table was a mug with the words printed on it 'Grow where you are planted!' That spoke to me. I asked the Lord to help me to be willing to go wherever he sent me. One day I had a strong feeling that if I was offered a job I should accept it, and not ask questions. When I was still researching the book I was approached by the patron of Rushere Hospital, in Ankole District, South West Uganda, to see if I would be willing to take on the administration of this hospital. After my previous reluctance to go where the Lord wanted me, I felt I should agree to take on this task. It never crossed my mind that I would still be there five and a half years later, and well into my 'retirement'.

Rushere Hospital

I had been to the area many years previously, sometimes on evangelistic safaris with other Christians, and at other times to visit parents of the students who were studying where I was headmistress. But I had never seen the hospital, nor did I know that I would be given a house and would have to make all the arrangements that involves. As my belongings were in the U.K., I rang Alice, a Ugandan friend, to see if she could lend me some kitchen equipment, cutlery, pillows, bedding and so on. Then I discovered that the mosquito netting on the windows was inadequate. Rushere Hospital is very rural and the few shops there don't run to mosquito netting. So in addition to kitchen and household basics, I asked Alice to bring mosquito netting and a carpenter to put it up! 'Would you like me to bring you someone who can help you in the house?' she enquired, over the phone. Would I! Grace duly arrived, and what a lovely lady she is. She still shares my home and looks after me wonderfully well.

What did I find when I looked round the hospital? I found a hospital block, three senior staff houses, several incomplete junior staff houses and a small farm. But there was no running water. A hospital with no running water, and meant-to-be flushing loos with no water connected to them, were probably the major problems. I declared that when water was laid on I would throw every bucket down the hill in jubilation! Every day the ailing pick-up truck brought yellow jerry-cans full of water up the hill to our houses from the bore hole in the hospital grounds. There was no electricity either, although there was a mains electricity transformer in the grounds. Nor was there a consistently functioning telephone in the area, and no mobile networks. We were very cut off.

I well remember the first day I went down into the hospital. I looked at John 10:3 'He calls his own sheep by name and leads them out,' and prayed for the Lord's presence and direction and peace, asking him to 'lead me out'. The staff had become so discouraged as the financial basis was inadequate, and there were therefore few patients. Morale was very low, with the consequent lack of trust and confidence from the people in the area. Almost as soon as I arrived voluntary morning prayers were started in the Out Patients for staff and patients as well as carers and visitors. That was an encouragement to us, and it continues to be so. Initially we had prayers from Monday to Friday, but the patients asked us why we did not have them daily. We now do.

Immediate answer to prayer

One of the first things that I felt I should tackle was the store, as equipment was piled up in corridors. 'She'll never manage it,' some said. Having told people in Kampala of my need of a store-keeper, I prayed, 'Lord, you know where I am, and you know my need of someone to help sort out the store.' The very next morning at around 10 a.m., a young man turned up and said, 'I have been a store-keeper and I believe you need help.' What an answer to prayer! Gradually the stores were sorted out. Not all answers to prayer are so instantaneous.

I knew a little of the hospital's interesting history. The area had been ridden with tsetse fly, and as long as that was the case neither people nor cattle could live there. In about 1960 the area was sprayed, and the Banyankore people arrived. Some were traders, but most were dairy farmers with their long-horned Ankole cattle. The majority had been semi-nomadic prior to settling there. Houses, schools, churches, shops and murram roads were built. But there was no medical work. As a result of requests from the people of the area the patron, who is a local landowner, agreed to purchase land and build the hospital.

God of miracles
Soon after starting work at the hospital, I went to Kampala and attended the Wednesday early morning Leader's Prayer Meeting. I heard one gentleman say that his name was Mr Timmins Jnr. Although I am very poor at remembering names, I thought I had read that name in a paper about the hospital. Was I right? Should I pluck up courage and ask him if he had ever heard of Rushere Hospital? I did, and imagine my delight when he told me that he had built it! Later we met again, and he explained that the hospital had been built on the understanding that it would have a Christian foundation. I had known nothing of that at all.

Without doubt we serve a God of miracles, and my time here has reminded me of that over and over again. Water is now laid on, and we have mains electricity. We work hand in hand with the Ministry of Health, and they have financed a maternity block, an operating theatre and a ward. Well-wishers from Uganda and elsewhere have helped us to build a lovely guest house. They have also built a house for the Director as well as enabling us to have running water in the hospital and in our houses. And our mobile phones and e-mail keep us in touch with the outside world. We still cannot use the Internet and we have to access e-mail through our mobile phones.

I thank the Lord that I have never doubted that he put me at the hospital. It has been hard work, but we have seen his hand on what has happened here in so many ways. I have frequently wondered why I am in Rushere, but I am learning that God is working his purposes out and that I do not need to understand everything. I thank the Lord for this most unexpected 'retirement' and for all those who have supported this challenging work. I am so grateful to the staff of the hospital and their tireless efforts, for Ministry officials, and for friends near and far. The Rwanda Mission's U.K. Committee is a constant support, as are 'Global Links', that is those who support us from outside Uganda. 'To God be the glory, great things he has done!'

10.

Frank and Helen Hamilton

After serving in the army during the Korean War, Frank was stationed at Governor's Island, New York. One weekend he visited his sister, who lived across the river in New Jersey, and she arranged a blind date for him. It turned out to be me, and we were married ten months later. Frank worked as a truck driver for the first ten years of our marriage while I stayed home with our children. We had five children in eight years so they kept me busy. However, I still managed to work part-time between births while my mother baby-sat for the first two. We needed additional income and I loved secretarial work, and did that plus book-keeping later in life.

I had joined the church as a teenage member of a confirmation class, although I don't think I really knew Christ personally until I was married and alone with the children. When Frank drove long distances, and was away much of the time, I became very nervous and cried at night then read my Bible, looking to the Lord for strength. God gave me the strength I needed and he has been my comfort and guide ever since. We both thought we were Christians when we married. But, years later, when we were living in Florida, I was asked to join a class to learn to share my faith and I realized I didn't know how. That showed me very clearly I needed to rededicate my life to Christ. When I did, my Saviour then became more real to me.

Frank, however, seemed to be drifting away from his family, the church and the Lord. He was becoming a workaholic. He left the travelling job when we moved to Florida, but then he worked nights and didn't see the family much. He hated it and felt trapped. The children and I went to church without him, as he wouldn't come. I think he was angry with God. One Sunday evening, the pastor asked for prayer requests as he always did. Others made requests and I kept waiting. I finally got the nerve to slip up my hand and ask them to pray for my husband to come to the Lord, and come back to the church and his family. I wanted help so badly that I knew I had to grab that opportunity.

Answered prayer
Two days later, Frank decided to take the day off work and went for a drive, taking along his Bible and a thermos of water. He parked on a deserted airplane runway in Boca

Raton, Florida, and looked up everything he could find on prayer. Then he prayed for forgiveness and asked the Lord to take over his life. From that day on he was a different person! He began to want to pray before meals and read the Scripture afterwards. The kids all wanted to know what was going on and I told them to rejoice with me. I remember saying, 'Hey, don't quench the Spirit!'

Frank witnessed to the men on the dock at work. Some thought he was nuts, but others were believers and welcomed him into their Bible studies and fellowship. He yearned to work days so he could attend church activities in the evenings. He was still unhappy about working nights. We asked the Lord to provide a daytime job. About a week after we began to pray about it, he had a call from the company's home office in Atlanta, Georgia. They needed a daytime dispatcher there. We discussed it, prayed some more, then decided that it was of the Lord, and away Frank went with our little camper. We put our house up for sale and I gave my notice to my employer. Just two weeks later, however, even though the job was going smoothly, the company was forced to send him back to Florida. They had lost a million dollars in the first quarter of the year and each division had to cut back one man. Frank was it, and back he came!

As he still had his old job and his dislike of the night-time work, we decided that maybe the Lord wanted us to move. We sold our house in a week – and the buyers had cash! The only stipulation was that we were to be out by 1st June. That was difficult since our son, Russell was graduating from high school on 10th June, and our son, Richard was getting married on 15th June. However, we agreed to the sale and moved to a furnished apartment for two weeks. We put all of our furniture in storage and just kept what we absolutely needed. Our plan was to take a trip across the country in order that Frank could show us what he had seen in his travels as a long distance driver. The idea was that he would look for work as we travelled.

We said goodbye to our dear friends at the church in Florida, loaded up our little camper, and away we went. We had three children with us. Russell had signed up to join the Air Force, but did not have to report for about two months, so he came along as well as Robert and Elizabeth, our teenage children who were still at home. Our oldest girl, Nancy, decided to remain in Florida with her job and her friends, and Richard went back to the Air Force base with his bride. We travelled 11,000 miles in sixty days, ending up at an evangelistic conference in North Carolina where Frank felt and accepted the call of the Lord to go into Christian service. We had no home, but we did have a destination. He would attend Reformed Theological Seminary in Jackson, Mississippi, for four years instead of the usual three, as he was forty-five years old and had never gone to college. Frank was accepted because of the Grandfather Clause, which provided for this situation. After sixty days on the road, we finally got out of the camper and into a house of our own and a new life began.

Four wonderful years

Seminary life, which lasted from 1978 till 1982, was wonderful. We met and became friends with about eight couples who were in the same position as we were. God had also called them later in life, and he used us oldies to minister to the younger couples on the campus. Many were newlyweds and just beginning raising their families. I think they looked up to us for advice and comfort. Frank studied hard. It wasn't easy since he had been away from schooling for a long time. In his last two years he was given preaching assignments and improved with experience. Upon graduation, he looked for a pulpit ministry and one came designed just for him. The First Presbyterian Church of Water Valley, Mississippi was seeking a pastor. They were going through a difficult time and needed an older man to lead them. Frank worked with each person, and through him the Holy Spirit brought harmony to the church once more.

Three years later we began to feel the tug of the Lord to move on. It was as if we were needed somewhere else. Two churches were interested in us, as was an alcohol rehabilitation centre. It was a difficult decision, but Frank felt the need to serve at the rehabilitation centre and he was accepted as Executive Director. Off we went to Boone, North Carolina for a period of two years. Frank preached eleven times a week in addition to directing, and I did the book-keeping and shopping. We had about forty people to feed and care for and we were very stressed. However, it was a most rewarding ministry as we saw many lives changed for the better. Then another job opened up in South Carolina for a director of a rehabilitation centre, and we moved once more. It seemed as though we were always moving! In Frank's earlier days he worked as a moving man so he was very experienced in packing and moving furniture. God had provided that training! This was a smaller facility but still very time consuming. After two fruitful years there, Frank was called to preach at a church in Andrews, North Carolina, that was looking for a pastor. Were we to move again? Yes! But it was worth unpacking that time as we stayed nine years. We loved the people and the community and put our roots down for good, we thought! Our two youngest children settled in Andrews also, and the other children visited from time to time.

The land of our roots

Nearing retirement and our fortieth wedding anniversary in 1995, we celebrated with a trip to Scotland to see the land of our roots. We loved the country and the people and really enjoyed ourselves. However, we were saddened by the lack of spirituality there. Scotland was formerly known as 'the land of the Book' and only a tiny percent of the people go to church now. Frank came home with a burden to work on the mission field in Scotland. It soon rubbed off on me, and we proceeded to search for ways to make this possible. So much for retirement! We visited many churches to raise support, telling them of our burden for Scotland. In about nine months we had raised enough to allow us to begin our work. We were in touch with many people in Scotland to determine how and where we could work. The Lord led us to Rev. David Robertson of St Peter's Free Church in Dundee. He suggested many things, but none of them worked out. Finally he said, 'Just come over and work for me!' That was what we did, although the Lord had things for us to do outside of St Peter's as well as inside the congregation.

We arrived on 13th February 1998 and went to David's home, where we stayed for a few days while we hunted for a place to live. God provided a cottage in Longforgan, a nearby village, and a car at a reasonable price. We were ready to begin, and almost immediately Frank found himself preaching. The church in our village often needed someone to fill the pulpit. Actually, there are four churches in the area served by one minister and an assistant. The minister preached at one at 9.30 a.m. then he rushed off to the next one that began at 11 a.m. The assistant did the same thing at the other two churches. We discovered this was very common in Scotland. We were glad that Frank was able to help them with their commitments.

Not long after we arrived, I heard about an International Women's Bible Study that was held in Dundee. The group certainly was international. We had several ladies from China, one from Argentina, another from Africa, and myself from America. Dundee is a university town, and most of these women had come to Scotland with their husbands who were attending the university. They wanted to learn what the Bible was all about, and I was one of those there who was more than willing to try to help them discover God's Word. Of course, as the group met in Scotland, we had tea, coffee and biscuits at our meetings. Nothing happens in Scotland without a kettle being put on to boil!

A neighbour invited us to a Bible Study in the city, and as we wanted to take every opportunity we could to be missionaries in Scotland, we decided to go along. Eight or nine people met in their lunch break to study God's Word. Before the study started someone stood outside in the street handing out tracts and inviting people in. There was also a sign out on the pavement (that's what Scots call the sidewalk) inviting in passers-by. From time to time people saw the notice or accepted a tract and invitation and came in and joined in the study. We think that meetings like that have a real place in evangelism as people have an hour to spare in the middle of their working day and God can use that time to challenge them.

Hobby cum outreach
Sewing is one of my hobbies and God even used that to open up a missionary opportunity. One day I saw a sign advertising a monthly quilting class in a Dundee church. I went along and enjoyed being around people with the same interests as myself. A while later one of the city churches employed a quilting buddie of mine to teach crafts as a way

of reaching out to the area around the church. She asked if I would go along to teach quilting. The five or six ladies who attended were not churchgoers, so it really was a way of reaching out to the community. We made two quilts that year and donated them to a nursing home. We had a ceremony at the home and got our picture in the paper! Of course we had tea and coffee as we sewed. It was no wonder that I gained weight in Scotland!

In the Fall of 1998, we heard that Franklin Graham was coming to Perth for a crusade in May the next year. It was to be called a festival rather than a crusade. I think they felt that more people would attend a festival. Frank was asked to be on the organizing committee and he ended up with the job of training all the counsellors. Churches were asked to schedule training sessions, then trainers were taught to lead the sessions. We went to Pitlochry for a weekend in December 1998 where we met many others from around the country who were also helping. It takes many people to organize a festival, and Frank seemed to be as involved as any of them.

When the church training schedule was published, we found we were teaching from Sunday through to Thursday each week. There just were not enough trainers. As Frank presented each lesson, I was busy preparing the next one. It was hard work keeping up! At one point we were in church twelve days in a row! We had counsellors' trainings Sunday through Thursday (each night in a different church). Then we had a Communion week-end with its services every evening, before we started off the training sessions for the next week on the Sunday night! And they call the senior years retirement!

Far too quickly the time for the Festival came round. There were big crowds and it was all very exciting. Frank was made 'trouble-shooter'. He equipped people with walkie-talkies and had to receive all their calls and help sort out their problems. Many people travelled a long way to be there, and a lot of people made professions of faith, both at the evening services and at the children's meetings. It was a bit like being back home for us because it was so American. But some of us felt it was too American, and should have included more Scottish hymns, guests and speakers. That's the kind of thing we would never have thought of before we left the States. Although God really blessed the Festival, and we were glad and privileged to be part of it, we were relieved when it was over. One of the things about taking on a new area of work in retirement is that you get tired more quickly than you used to do. By the end of the Franklin Graham Festival we were tired, like, very tired. Despite that both Frank and I feel that working at the Festival was one of the reasons God took us to Scotland.

Work with prisoners

During the Festival training sessions, I heard about a need for helpers at the Prison Fellowship's Drop-in Kitchen in one of Dundee's downtown churches. I became a regular helper there, and Frank was invited along to lead the devotions when the people heard that he was a pastor from the States. Although most of those who came were walk-ins from the street, some ex-prisoners did attend. On the subject of prisons, we were asked to teach a course to some selected prisoners in Perth Prison. We used the same teaching material as we used for Festival counsellors, though prisoners weren't, of course, able to be counsellors. Much to my surprise, some of them were allowed to attend the Festival.

Longforgan, where we lived, is situated next to the village of Castle Huntly. There is actually a castle there, but it is used as an open prison for men on a work-release programme. There are no locks on the doors and people are trusted not to leave the place. Men go there during the last year of their sentences in order to acclimatize them to the free world. Each morning they walked into Longforgan where they caught the bus to their places of employment, and we would see them returning at the end of the working day. Occasionally we heard of men who didn't return. When they were caught they went to Perth Prison rather than back to Castle Huntly, and some additional time was added to their sentence, I think. Frank taught a Festival course in the prison and also led a weekly Bible study there for eight weeks.

Mission trips

Another thing we were involved in was arranging mission trips from the States. One of them was called the Agape Puppets. They came and put on shows with a gospel message. It took a lot of time to make plans for where they could perform over their ten-day visit, and where they would stay. Eventually churches and schools invited the Agape Puppets and they went down very well. It was hard work, as Frank transported the team around and we fed them every night. Thankfully I like cooking! When people asked me about our time as missionaries in Scotland, I don't know what they expected me to tell them. But the Agape Puppets story is as good a one as any. We had to find a large van for the duration of their stay as they carry their puppet theatre in a long ski bag and their twenty puppets in two large suitcases. That's what they bring, but they don't take it all away again, because they leave the equipment behind them in order that local people can continue using it to spread the gospel, especially among children and young people. Agape Puppets have travelled the world, doing shows in Russia, China, Mexico, Africa, South America, Ireland, and now Scotland. God has really blessed their unusual ministry.

Although we were based in St Peter's Church, we found that the Lord had work for us to do in all sorts of places. For example, the man who lent us a van when the Agape Puppets were with us, asked us to help cook for a camp for underprivileged children. It was about an hour from home at a Boy Scouts' campsite. As we were not as young as we used to be, we decided to sleep at home and go every day to help cook the meal then clear up after it. The kids wanted to hear our 'funny' accents and they asked us so many questions! That gave us great opportunities to tell them about the Lord and how he had brought us to Scotland. 'Why would anyone want to leave America and come here?' one boy asked us. He was quite serious. These kids saw the American way of life on television and thought it was marvellous. They knew much more about America than kids in the States know about Scotland, and they are much more interested. If talking about America allowed us to say a little about the Lord, we were all for talking!

Pensioners all!

One of the activities in St Peter's that was dear to our hearts grew out of a team visiting from Mississippi. While they were there, we were asked to plan a pensioners' lunch as a means of outreach. We did that, and served soup and sandwiches to the people who came. It worked so well that the church decided to continue it, and Frank and I were given the job as supervisors. We met monthly, and the number of pensioners who attended grew as time went on. Frank collected people from a local nursing home too. We put on a programme or had a speaker each month. Two ladies from the congregation made soup and I bought the rest and made cookies. Volunteers helped us set up tables, make the sandwiches and clear up afterwards. The pensioners (we were pensioners ourselves!) stayed a while before we took them home, though some from nearby just walked.

We lived in Scotland for four years, and would have stayed there forever if it had not been for the tug of family at home and the need for some health attention. By the time we left, Frank was sixty-nine years old and having heart problems. Although he was being well treated by the National Health Service, we felt that he needed to see his cardiologist in the States for long-term care. We prayed about staying, but the answer came that it was time to go home.

The people of Scotland poured out their hearts to us with so much love. St Peter's gave us a really special going-away party, and friends sent us gifts and cards to remember them by. We had never been treated so royally! It was hard to leave such wonderful people. But, having made our decision, we packed our things and headed home over the Atlantic. Frank and I often talk about going back to visit Scotland, and I believe we will one day. But Frank's health prevents us from returning to work on the mission field. We bought a home in our beloved Andrews, North Carolina, and thought we would settle down at last. However, we are now working again, but only part-time in our son's business. Frank runs the office and I keep the books. The secretary moved out of town not long after we returned! Frank leads a Wednesday night Bible study and preaches whenever needed. It seems there is no such word as retirement in our vocabulary. Perhaps one day it will emerge, and that will be okay; but if it doesn't, that's okay too.

FURTHER INFORMATION

For further information on organizations mentioned in the book contact:

Fergus Macdonald
Scottish Bible Society
Bible House, 7 Hampton Terrace,
Edinburgh EH12 5XU
Website: www.scottishbiblesociety.org
United Bible Society
World Service Centre, 7th Floor,
Reading Bridge House,
Reading, RG6 8PJ
Email: comms@ubs-wsc.org
Website: www.biblesociety.org

David and Joyce Moffett
United World Mission

9401-B Southern Pines Boulevard, Charlotte,
North Carolina 28273-5596
Website: www.uwm.org
London City Mission
175 Tower Bridge Road, London, SE1 2AA
Website: www.lcm.org.uk

Jim Cromarty
Presbyterian Church of Eastern Australia
Email: jac@pcea.asn.au
Website: www.pcea.asn.au

Thomas Bowen
Chamberlain-Hunt Academy
124 McComb Avenue, Port Gibson,
Mississippi 39159
Website: www.chamberlain-hunt.com

Matthew and Muriel McKinnon
Mission Aviation Fellowship
1) Challenge House, Canal Street, Glasgow, G4 0AD
   Email: maf-scot.off@maf-uk.org
2) Castle Hill Avenue, Folkestone, Kent, CT20 2TN
   Email: maf@maf-uk.org
   Website: www.maf-uk.org
3) 1849 N. Wabash Avenue, Redlands, California 92374
   Email: maf-us@maf.org

Tearfund
100 Church Road,
TEDDINGTON TW11 8QE
Email: enquiry@tearfund.org
Website: www.tearfund.org

Ed Forrester
The Good News Jail and Prison Ministry
    2230 E. Parham Road, Richmond, Virginia 23228.
    Email: info@goodnewsjail.org

Peter Morrison
Free Church of Scotland International Board
    The Mound, Edinburgh, EH1 2LS
    Website: www.freechurch.org

Joan Hall
Rushere Hospital in Uganda
    Miss J Preston, Tan Y Coed, Mawddwy, Machynlleth,
    Achynlleth, SY20 9LN
    Email: sianpreston@talk21.com
    Website: www.rusherehospital.com

Frank and Helen Hamilton
Mission to the World
    1600 North Brown Road, Lawrenceville,
    Georgia 30043-8141

Other books
of interest from
_____

Christian Focus Publications

A New Biography of
HUDSON TAYLOR

IT IS NOT
DEATH
TO DIE

Jim Cromarty

It is not Death to Die

A New biography of Hudson Taylor

Jim Cromarty

Hudson Taylor's philosophy was simple

> 'There is a living God,
> He has spoken in the Bible.
> He means what he says,
> and will do all that he has promised.'

Hudson Taylor's life is one that should encourage Christians to step out in faith to fulfil the commands of God. His life's work was motivated by a love of God and a love of his fellow man. His heart's desire was to see Christ glorified in people coming to faith, particularly the Chinese.

Encouraged by another missionary, W.C. Burns, Hudson changed western dress and imperialistic attitudes for Chinese ways. He served, and still serves, as a model for mission work around the world.

He led an extraordinary life and Jim Cromarty has succeeded in capturing the thrill of his pioneering work. It is as if we too are able to step outside the comfortable boundaries most of us never come close to exploring beyond.

Jim Cromarty is an Australian minister and has written other successful biographies and family devotional books.

ISBN 1-85792-632-3

LIGHT IN THE CITY
Stories from LONDON CITY MISSION
IRENE HOWAT

'A good read, full of human interest.' Maureen McKenna

Light in the City

Stories from London City Mission

Edited By Irene Howat

A set of testimonies with a difference. Central are the stories of London City Missionaries. Their experiences before conversion were varied and include: **alcohol and drug abuse, sexual abuse, racial issues, poverty, violence, involvement in cults such as Rastafarianism, Jehovah Witnesses and the occult**.

Alongside these are stories of people who have come to faith through the work of LCM, interspersed with some shorter accounts of people who have been challenged with the gospel but who have not yet accepted it. Together, they illustrate the work of the Mission and their care for those whom they meet.

'God took ordinary men and women, some of whom faced big problems in their own lives, and saved them. Their stories are fascinating, their work is a slog but it's never dull.'

**The late Maureen McKenna,
Founder of the Open Door Trust, Glasgow**

This book ends with a short explanation of the Christian Faith using answers to the sort of questions that LCM missionaries are asked every day at work.

ISBN 1-85792-723-0

MIRACLES *from* MAYHEM

THE STORY OF MAY NICHOLSON

IRENE HOWAT

Miracles from Mayhem

The Story of May Nicholson

Irene Howat

'Anyone who has lived with drug addicts and alcoholics knows how elusive hope is. It runs through your fingers like fine sand, until there's nothing left but cynicism and despair. But May Nicholson found a different sort of hope - rather, it found her! Her encounter with Jesus Christ literally "saved" her life, and set in motion what one of her colleagues calls 'a friendly steamroller' - clearing paths of hope not just for herself but for dozens and dozens of others too.'

John Nicholls, London City Mission

'May has the same love for the poorest of the poor and the richest of the rich. She is at home with lords and ladies and with the lowly and loneliest. Living out God's love with and among the poor, she reflects Jesus who, "though he was rich, yet for your sake he became poor that we might be made rich".'

Chuck Wright

May Nicholson was a notorious fighting drunk until her conversion when she was 34. The last 22 years have been spent tirelessly working for the Lord as an outreach worker in Paisley, Dundee and Glasgow's Govan.

This book tells a remarkable story of a life completely changed and transformed by God.

ISBN 1-85792-897-0

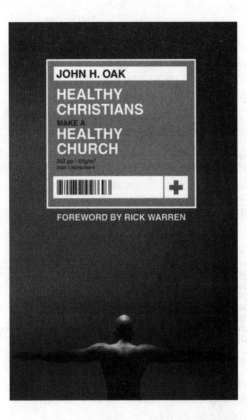

JOHN H. OAK

HEALTHY
CHRISTIANS
MAKE A
HEALTHY
CHURCH

352 pp · 60g/m²
ISBN 1-84550-694-4

FOREWORD BY RICK WARREN

Healthy Christians make a Healthy Church

John H. Oak

Foreword by Rick Warren

'The starting point in leading members to maturity is to invest time in teaching your members what the Bible says about these issues. You must lay the biblical foundation. Teach it in classes, sermons, seminars, home cell groups and every other way you can emphasise it. You should never stop teaching on the importance of every Christian having a ministry. This book can be your guide.'

Rick Warren,
Saddleback Community Church, California

'Sarang Community Church is huge and still growing; and it is also solidly orthodox and Reformed. I commend this book to any individual who desires to understand the biblical principles of building a church...'

Samuel Logan,
Westminster Theological Seminary, Philadelphia

'...the people of the church are not called to assist pastors in their ministry. Rather pastors are called to assist the people in their ministry, and to do it by intentional equipping. While written in the context of a mega-church, the discipleship model of leadership development is timeless, and timely, applicable to a church of a hundred or a thousand. This book and its author, are gifts to the people of God everywhere.'

R. Paul Stevens,
Regent College, Vancouver

John H. Oak started Sarang Community Church in 1978 with a handful and it is now one of the largest Presbyterian Churches in the world with 30,000 members.

ISBN 1-85792-869-5

UNSEARCHABLE RICHES

Invest in a Relationship that lasts an Eternity

Vernon Higham

Unsearchable Riches

Invest in a relationship that lasts an Eternity

Vernon Higham

In a small, but meaty, book, Vernon Higham takes us through some fundamental truths of the Christian gospel so that others will find evidence of God's work in our lives (not just our words!). Higham skilfully expresses the Christian 'world-view' and enables us to put belief into action in surprisingly effective ways.

A special feature is a section at the end of each chapter where he applies the theology in practical and encouraging ways. We have no excuse for our daily life to not be affected and effective!

This book that has two great uses – It is a useful tool for helping Christians articulate their faith to non-Christians and it is a great gift for someone seeking to know more about God.

'A warm, easy-to-read introduction to key Bible doctrines... a great help to many people.'

Eryl Davies,
Evangelical Theological College of Wales

Vernon Higham was pastor of Heath Evangelical Church, in Cardiff from 1962 until he retired in September 2002. His has also written 'God's Workmanship' ISBN 1-85792-255-7.

ISBN 1-85792-768-0

Christian Focus Publications
publishes books for all ages

Our mission statement –

STAYING FAITHFUL

In dependence upon God we seek to help make His infallible Word, the Bible, relevant. Our aim is to ensure that the Lord Jesus Christ is presented as the only hope to obtain forgiveness of sin, live a useful life and look forward to heaven with Him.

REACHING OUT

Christ's last command requires us to reach out to our world with His gospel. We seek to help fulfil that by publishing books that point people towards Jesus and help them develop a Christ-like maturity. We aim to equip all levels of readers for life, work, ministry and mission.

Books in our adult range are published in three imprints.

Christian Focus contains popular works including biographies, commentaries, basic doctrine and Christian living. Our children's books are also published in this imprint.

Mentor focuses on books written at a level suitable for Bible College and seminary students, pastors, and other serious readers. The imprint includes commentaries, doctrinal studies, examination of current issues and church history.

Christian Heritage contains classic writings from the past.

Christian Focus Publications Ltd,
Geanies House, Fearn, Tain,
Ross-shire, IV20 1TW, Scotland, United Kingdom
info@christianfocus.com
www.christianfocus.com